PACEMAKER® PRACTICAL ARITHMETIC SERIES

Working Makes Sense

Charles H. Kahn

J. Bradley Hanna

GLOBE FEARON

PACEMAKER® PRACTICAL ARITHMETIC SERIES

Money Makes Sense

Using Dollars and Sense

Working Makes Sense

Buying with Sense

CONTENTS

Director of Editorial and Marketing, Special Education: Diane Galen
Marketing Manager: Susan McLaughlin
Assistant Marketing Manager: Donna Frasco
Executive Editor: Joan Carrafiello
Senior Editor: Stephanie Petron Cahill
Contributing Editor: Jennifer McCarthy
Editorial Assistant: Brian Hawkes
Production Director: Kurt Scherwatzky
Production Editor: John Roberts
Art Supervision: Pat Smythe
Cover Design: A Good Thing Inc.
Interior Design: Thompson Steele Production Services
Electronic Page Production: Thompson Steele Production Services
Illustrators: Thompson Steele Production Services, Teresa Camozzi,
         and Sam Masami Daijogo

ISBN 0-835-93465-9

Printed in the United States of America

8 9 10 11 12   05 04

1-800-321-3106
www.pearsonlearning.com

Why do you think people work? "To make money," you might answer. You would be right. Most people must work to earn a living.

By working, you earn the money you need to live on your own. You earn money for things you need, like food and clothes. You earn money to pay your bills. You also earn money to buy the things you want. Making money is a good reason for working. Making money is one reason that working makes sense.

There is more to working than just making money. There are other good reasons for working, too. Work can be hard. At the end of the day, you may feel tired but proud. You will feel good inside knowing that you have done your work well. No matter what kind of work you do, you have a right to feel important. Doing a good job is one of the most important things that anyone can do. It is another reason working makes sense.

When you work, you use money almost every day.
When you use your money, you need skills in addition,
subtraction, multiplication, and division.

This book will help you learn the skills you need to use
the money you earn. You will learn to use decimals.
You will also learn about percents and fractions. You
will learn about savings and checking accounts, too.
These new skills will help you to use the money you
earn wisely. By using your earnings wisely, you will
see that working makes sense.

Answer these questions about working.

1. Suppose you work from 8:00 A.M. to 4:30 P.M. each
   day. You take one hour off for lunch. How many
   hours do you work each day?   _____

2. Suppose you earn $6.00 an hour. If you work
   8 hours, how much money will you earn?   _____

   If you work 40 hours, how much money will
   you earn?   _____

3. Suppose you earn $5.50 an hour. How much money
   will you earn for working $6\frac{1}{2}$ hours?   _____

4. When you work more than 40 hours a week, you
   are paid time and a half. If you earn $5.50 an hour
   for regular time, how much will you earn for one
   hour of overtime?   _____

5. You earn $850 in one month. If you save $\frac{1}{8}$ of it,
   how much money will you save?   _____

6. You have $65.00 in your savings account. If your
   money earns 5% interest each year, how much
   money will you have altogether after one year?   _____

7. Every week you drive a total of 98 miles to and from
   work. Your car uses 3.5 gallons of gas for these trips.
   How many miles per gallon does the car get?   _____

8. Suppose you earn $866.00 a month. You are given
   a 15% raise. How much will you make a month now?   _____

Work these problems on checking accounts.

9. Write out this check to Fiesta Foods for $78.16. Use today's date and sign your name.

NUMBER 209

01-05 / 638

_____ 19 ____

PAY TO THE ORDER OF _____ $ _____

_____ DOLLARS
nonnegotiable

CITIZEN'S BANK
Barrington, Oklahoma

_____

⑈0638⑈ 01051: 34 1297 2⑈

10. Complete this checkbook register. Figure the new balance for each check written and each deposit. *Subtract* the checks and *add* the deposits. You may use a calculator to complete the register.

CHECK NO.	DATE	CHECKS ISSUED TO OR DESCRIPTION OF DEPOSIT	AMOUNT OF CHECK		✔	AMOUNT OF DEPOSIT		BALANCE	
								416	09
209	5/10	Fiesta Foods (groceries)	78	16					
210	5/12	Dr. Frank (dentist bill)	45	00					
211	5/12	Gant's Dept. Store (clothes)	54	98					
—	5/15	deposit				447	29		
212	5/18	Super Oil Co. (gas)	67	76					
213	5/20	Franklin Garage (oil change)	17	84					
214	5/21	Graham Telephone (telephone bill)	45	19					
215	5/21	Entropy Power Co. (electric bill)	28	30					
216	5/24	West Bank (car payment)	225	00					
—	5/31	deposit				387	29		
217	5/31	Hillcrest Apartments (rent)	550	00					
218	5/31	United Charge-It-All (credit card)	39	63					

NAME _____

Find the answers to these arithmetic problems.

1.
```
   67
   79
   86
 + 42
```

2.
```
  $3.95
 - 1.82
```

3.
```
  $26.46
 ×     7
```

4.
```
  $72.95
 - 31.64
```

5. $4\overline{)256}$

6.
```
  $8.31
   6.50
 + .38
```

7. $6.4\overline{)72}$

8.
```
  $314.06
 -  71.48
```

9.
```
  $128.45
 ×    .06
```

10.
```
  $379.42
 - 226.37
```

11. $12\overline{)104.76}$

12.
```
  $82.84
 - 69.32
```

13.
```
  $87.30
 ×    49
```

14.
```
  $6.61
   8.37
   4.55
 + 3.19
```

15.
```
  $6.97
 ×   38
```

16. 3)$8.25

17. $714.00
        × .31

18. $841.93
       − 638.67

19. $983.42
         766.11
       + 353.64

20. 1.5)12.9

21. Find 7% of $12.00. _____

22. Find 10% of $318.00. _____

23. Find 14% of $33.25. _____

24. Find 50% of $426.36. _____

25. Find 75% of $23.04. _____

26. Find $\frac{3}{8}$ of 136 lbs. _____

27. Find $\frac{1}{2}$ of $13.26. _____

28. Find $\frac{1}{4}$ of 36.4 lbs. _____

29. Find $\frac{2}{3}$ of $114.72. _____

30. Find $\frac{3}{4}$ of $51.96. _____

Carla Williams was looking for a part-time job after school. She saw an ad in the newspaper for Runaway Sports Shop. They needed someone to work evenings and weekends. Carla went to the store and filled out an application. She had an interview with the store manager, Mr. Swift. He told Carla about the work she would be doing. He also told her the pay and hours for the job. Carla thought the job sounded good. Mr. Swift thought Carla would make a good employee, so she was hired.

The day Carla started her job, Mr. Swift showed her how to use the time clock. "Many stores, offices, and factories have time clocks," Mr. Swift said. "A time clock makes it easy to keep a record of the hours you work. You stamp your time card in the clock when you start work. You stamp it again when you stop work. The time card shows the hours you worked."

Here is Carla's time card for the first week she worked. From Monday through Friday, Carla worked evenings from 5:00 P.M. to 9:00 P.M. On Saturday, she worked from 9:00 A.M. to 6:00 P.M., with 1 hour off for lunch. Write on Carla's time card the number of hours she worked each day. Then add to find the total number of hours she worked that week.

1.

DAY	A.M.		P.M.		HOURS
	IN	OUT	IN	OUT	
Sunday					
Monday			5:00	9:00	
Tuesday			5:00	9:00	
Wednesday			5:00	9:00	
Thursday			5:00	9:00	
Friday			5:00	9:00	
Saturday	9:00	12:00	1:00	6:00	
				Total Hours	

Carla did not always work the same number of hours each week. Here are Carla's time cards for the next two weeks. Write the number of hours Carla worked each day on her time card. Then add to find the total number of hours she worked each week.

2.

DAY	A.M.		P.M.		HOURS
	IN	OUT	IN	OUT	
Sunday					
Monday			5:00	9:00	
Tuesday			5:00	8:30	
Wednesday			5:00	9:00	
Thursday			5:00	8:30	
Friday			5:00	9:00	
Saturday	9:00	12:00	1:00	5:00	
				Total Hours	

3.

DAY	A.M.		P.M.		HOURS
	IN	OUT	IN	OUT	
Sunday					
Monday			5:00	8:00	
Tuesday			5:00	9:00	
Wednesday			5:00	8:30	
Thursday			5:00	9:00	
Friday			5:00	9:00	
Saturday	9:00	1:00	2:00	5:30	
				Total Hours	

Time Cards

Here are the time cards of some other people who work at Runaway Sports Shop. Figure out how many hours each person worked each day. Write the number of hours on the time card. Then add to find the total number of hours each person worked that week.

1.

DAY	A.M.		P.M.		HOURS
	IN	OUT	IN	OUT	
Sunday			12:00	6:00	
Monday	9:00	1:00	2:00	5:00	
Tuesday	9:00	1:00	2:00	4:30	
Wednesday	9:30	12:30	1:30	5:00	
Thursday	9:00	12:30	1:30	5:30	
Friday	9:00	1:00	2:00	5:30	
Saturday					
				Total Hours	

2.

DAY	A.M.		P.M.		HOURS
	IN	OUT	IN	OUT	
Sunday					
Monday	10:00	12:00	1:00	4:30	
Tuesday	10:00	1:00	2:00	5:00	
Wednesday	10:30	12:00	1:00	5:00	
Thursday	10:00	12:30	1:30	4:30	
Friday	9:00	12:00	1:00	4:00	
Saturday					
				Total Hours	

3.

DAY	A.M.		P.M.		HOURS
	IN	OUT	IN	OUT	
Sunday			12:30	6:30	
Monday	9:30	12:30	1:30	5:00	
Tuesday	9:00	12:00	1:00	5:00	
Wednesday	9:00	12:30	1:30	4:30	
Thursday	9:00	12:00	1:00	5:30	
Friday					
Saturday			1:00	6:00	
				Total Hours	

Addition in Action

Find the answers to these addition problems.

1. 4 4 + 4 12	**2.** 6 4 + 5 15	**3.** 8 9 + 8	**4.** 7 6 + 6	**5.** 1 9 + 1
6. 7 3 3 + 5	**7.** 8 8 4 + 9	**8.** 6 4 5 + 7	**9.** 8 2 2 + 5	**10.** 6 7 3 + 6
11. 9 12 + 14	**12.** 23 6 + 15	**13.** 51 22 + 12	**14.** 86 15 + 14 115	**15.** 92 30 + 20
16. 77 9 18 + 18	**17.** 95 21 5 + 10	**18.** 65 37 20 + 14	**19.** 41 59 16 + 13	**20.** 17 83 24 + 42
21. 124 14 19 + 23	**22.** 112 20 215 + 15	**23.** 222 48 67 + 411	**24.** 534 215 46 + 94	**25.** 783 70 109 + 22
26. 224 315 79 + 3	**27.** 118 420 130 + 6	**28.** 93 444 127 + 27	**29.** 130 507 16 + 4	**30.** 642 199 7 + 38

Each week, Carla added up the hours on her time card. She used the total number of hours to figure out how much money she earned that week.

First she wrote down how much money she earned an hour. Carla was paid $5.25 an hour. For every hour she worked, she earned:

Then she multiplied that amount by the total number of hours she worked. Here is how she figured her earnings for one week.

$5.25 amount Carla was paid an hour
× 27 number of hours Carla worked
36.75
105.00
$141.75 amount of money Carla earned

Use Carla's time cards to figure out how much she earned each week. First figure out the total number of hours she worked. Then multiply the number of hours by the amount she earned each hour—$5.25. (Use the Multiplication Table on page 127 if you need help.) Be sure to put the decimal point in the right place in your answers.

1.

DAY	A.M.		P.M.		HOURS
	IN	OUT	IN	OUT	
Sunday					
Monday			5:00	9:00	
Tuesday			5:00	8:00	
Wednesday			5:00	8:30	
Thursday			5:00	9:00	
Friday			5:00	8:30	
Saturday	10:00	12:30	1:30	6:00	
				Total Hours	

Amount of money Carla earned: _____

2.

DAY	A.M.		P.M.		HOURS
	IN	OUT	IN	OUT	
Sunday					
Monday			4:30	9:00	
Tuesday			5:00	9:00	
Wednesday			5:00	8:30	
Thursday			5:00	9:00	
Friday			4:30	8:30	
Saturday	9:00	12:00	1:00	6:00	
				Total Hours	

Amount of money Carla earned: _____

3.

DAY	A.M.		P.M.		HOURS
	IN	OUT	IN	OUT	
Sunday					
Monday			5:00	9:00	
Tuesday			4:30	9:00	
Wednesday			5:00	8:30	
Thursday			5:00	8:30	
Friday			5:00	9:00	
Saturday	9:30	12:00	1:00	6:00	
				Total Hours	

Amount of money Carla earned: _____

4.

DAY	A.M.		P.M.		HOURS
	IN	OUT	IN	OUT	
Sunday					
Monday			5:00	9:00	
Tuesday			6:00	9:00	
Wednesday			5:30	9:00	
Thursday			5:00	8:30	
Friday			4:30	9:00	
Saturday	9:00	12:30	1:00	5:00	
				Total Hours	

Amount of money Carla earned: _____

Figuring Earnings

Here are the time cards of some other people who work at Runaway Sports Shop. The employees do not earn the same amount of money an hour.

Help them to figure out how much they earned each week. First figure out the total number of hours they worked. Then multiply the number of hours by the amount each employee earned an hour.

1. Mary Rossi earns $5.25 an hour.

DAY	A.M.		P.M.		HOURS
	IN	OUT	IN	OUT	
Sunday			12:00	6:00	
Monday	9:30	12:00	1:00	5:00	
Tuesday	9:30	12:30	1:30	5:00	
Wednesday					
Thursday	9:00	12:00	1:00	5:00	
Friday	9:30	12:00	1:00	5:30	
Saturday	9:00	12:00			
				Total Hours	

Amount of money Mary earned: _____

2. Ted Jenkins earns $6.50 an hour.

DAY	A.M.		P.M.		HOURS
	IN	OUT	IN	OUT	
Sunday			1:00	6:00	
Monday			4:30	9:00	
Tuesday			5:00	9:30	
Wednesday			5:00	9:00	
Thursday					
Friday					
Saturday	9:00	12:00	1:00	6:00	
				Total Hours	

Amount of money Ted earned: _____

3. Randy Sumo earns $5.50 an hour.

DAY	A.M.		P.M.		HOURS
	IN	OUT	IN	OUT	
Sunday					
Monday	9:00	12:00	12:30	5:30	
Tuesday	9:00	12:00	12:30	6:00	
Wednesday	9:30	12:00	1:00	6:30	
Thursday			12:30	5:30	
Friday	9:00	12:30	1:00	6:00	
Saturday					
				Total Hours	

Amount of money Randy earned: _____

4. David Weinberg earns $5.75 an hour.

DAY	A.M.		P.M.		HOURS
	IN	OUT	IN	OUT	
Sunday					
Monday			5:00	9:00	
Tuesday			5:30	9:00	
Wednesday	10:00	12:30	1:30	5:00	
Thursday	10:00	12:30	1:00	5:00	
Friday			5:00	9:00	
Saturday					
				Total Hours	

Amount of money David earned: _____

5. Sandy Jackson earns $6.00 an hour.

DAY	A.M.		P.M.		HOURS
	IN	OUT	IN	OUT	
Sunday					
Monday					
Tuesday	9:00	12:00	1:00	5:30	
Wednesday	9:00	12:00	12:30	5:00	
Thursday	9:30	12:30	1:30	6:30	
Friday	9:00	1:00	2:00	6:00	
Saturday	10:00	12:00	1:00	6:00	
				Total Hours	

Amount of money Sandy earned: _____

Figuring Earnings

Every week, Mr. Swift had to figure how much each of his employees had earned. First he wrote down how much the employee was paid an hour. Then he multiplied that amount by the number of hours the employee worked.

Help Mr. Swift figure how much each employee earned a week. Be sure to put the decimal point in the right place in your answers.

1. $5.50
    × 29
    4950
    1100
    $159.50

2. $6.25
    × 35

3. $5.75
    × 30

4. $5.65
    × 20

5. $5.90
    × 35

6. $6.50
    × 32

7. $7.00
    × 40

8. $5.85
    × 38

9. $5.45
    × 25

10. $5.85
    × 27

11. $6.00
    × 40

12. $7.50
    × 35

13. $5.40
    × 23

14. $6.25
    × 38

15. $5.50
    × 35

16. $10.00
    × 37

17. $5.65
    × 34

18. $6.10
    × 40

19. $6.50
    × 31

20. $5.65
    × 25

Multiplication in Action

Find the answers to these multiplication problems.
Be sure to put the decimal point in the right place.

1. $2.54
  × 8
  $20.32

2. $9.23
  × 6

3. $8.65
  × 12

4. $1.39
  × 43

5. $3.57
  × 29

6. $9.98
  × 37

7. $7.21
  × 54

8. $4.53
  × 23

9. $6.82
  × 35

10. $1.86
  × 67

11. $4.08
  × 71

12. $5.73
  × 26

13. $8.41
  × 82

14. $2.56
  × 13

15. $7.19
  × 96

16. $8.35
  × 24

17. $1.49
  × 32

18. $7.65
  × 98
  6120
  6885
  $749.70

19. $6.15
  × 75

20. $4.64
  × 59

21. $3.50
  × 62

22. $1.78
  × 89

23. $5.05
  × 48

24. $4.19
  × 16

25. $2.27
  × 41

26. $3.82
  × 83

27. $9.78
  × 56

28. $1.03
  × 87

29. $7.42
  × 64

30. $2.88
  × 21

Steve Pollard, one of Carla Williams's friends, also had a part-time job. He worked as a waiter at The Sandwich House. He was paid $5.50 an hour. One day he worked 4 hours. Here's how Steve figured his wages, or earnings, for that day.

$$\begin{array}{r} \$5.50 \\ \times\ 4 \\ \hline \$22.00 \end{array}$$ hourly wage / hours worked / wages earned

Sometimes the number of hours Steve worked did not come out as a whole number. One day he worked $4\frac{1}{2}$ hours. To figure his wages for $4\frac{1}{2}$ hours, Steve first multiplied his hourly wage by the number of full hours he worked.

$$\begin{array}{r} \$5.50 \\ \times\ 4 \\ \hline \$22.00 \end{array}$$ hourly wage / full hours worked / wages for 4 hours

To figure his wages for $\frac{1}{2}$ hour, he divided his hourly wage by 2.

$2.75 wages for $\frac{1}{2}$ hour

$$\begin{array}{r} 2\overline{)\$5.50} \\ \underline{4} \\ 1\,5\,0 \\ \underline{1\,4} \\ 1\,0 \\ \underline{1\,0} \end{array}$$

$$\begin{array}{r} \$22.00 \\ +\ 2.75 \\ \hline \$24.75 \end{array}$$ wages for 4 hours / wages for $\frac{1}{2}$ hour / wages for $4\frac{1}{2}$ hours

Then he added the two amounts together to find his total wages for the day.

Here are the hours Steve worked one week. How much did he earn in wages for each day? How much did he earn in wages for the week?

Day	Hours Worked	Wages Earned
Monday	4	$22.00
Tuesday	$4\frac{1}{2}$	_____
Wednesday	$3\frac{1}{2}$	_____
Thursday	$2\frac{1}{2}$	_____
Friday	3	_____
Saturday	$7\frac{1}{2}$	_____
	Total wages for the week	_____

Steve earned $5.25 an hour in wages. But he made more than that because he also got tips from the people he waited on. One day he worked 2 hours and made $19.15. How much did he get in tips that day?

You can use multiplication and subtraction to find out. First, figure how much Steve earned at $5.25 an hour.

$5.25	hourly wage
× 2	hours worked
$11.50	wages earned

Then, to find out how much Steve got in tips, subtract his wages from the total amount he made that day.

$19.15	total
−$11.50	wages earned
$ 7.65	tips

Here are Steve's hours and earnings for one week. Figure how much he made in tips each day. Then figure how much he made in tips for the whole week.

1.

Day	Hours Worked	Total Earned (wages and tips)	Tips
Monday	2	$19.15	$8.65
Tuesday	3	$24.90	_____
Wednesday	3	$26.55	_____
Thursday	2	$17.22	_____
Friday	4	$36.30	_____
Saturday	7	$60.95	_____
		Total tips	_____

Figure Steve's tips for the next week.

2.

Day	Hours Worked	Total Earned (wages and tips)	Tips
Monday	3	$30.00	_____
Tuesday	3	$23.65	_____
Wednesday	2	$15.45	_____
Thursday	2	$19.50	_____
Friday	4	$34.80	_____
Saturday	5	$42.15	_____
		Total tips	_____

Deductions

Carla Williams worked 28 hours her first week at Runaway Sports Shop. She earned $5.25 an hour. So she figured she had earned $147.00.

$$\begin{array}{r} \$ 5.25 \text{ hourly wage} \\ \times 28 \text{ hours worked} \\ \hline 4200 \\ 1050 \\ \hline \$147.00 \text{ earnings} \end{array}$$

But when Carla got her paycheck, she saw that it was made out for only $118.84. Carla asked Mr. Swift why she did not get all the money she had earned. Mr. Swift told Carla that four *deductions* had been taken from her paycheck. The amount of money of each deduction was listed on her paycheck.

DEDUCTIONS

GROSS WAGES	FEDERAL INCOME TAX	STATE INCOME TAX	FICA	MEDICARE	NET WAGES
$147.00	$11.60	$5.42	$9.03	$2.11	$118.84

Mr. Swift explained each thing listed on Carla's paycheck.

Gross wages   This is the amount you earn before any deductions.

Federal income tax   This deduction is used to help run the federal government. The amount taken depends on how much you make.

State income tax   This deduction is used to help run your state government. Some states do not have a state tax deduction. The amount taken depends on how much you make.

FICA   (Federal Insurance Contributions Act) The federal government uses the money from FICA deductions for your Social Security payments. You may receive a Social Security check each month if you meet the following requirements: 1) you retire after age 62, 2) your spouse dies, or 3) you meet certain medical requirements. The amount taken is a percent of your total wages.

Medicare   The federal government uses this money to pay for health care for some elderly and disabled persons. The amount taken is a percent of your total wages.

Net wages   This is the amount you take home after all deductions have been subtracted from your earnings. This amount is also called your *take-home pay*.

Find the net wages, or take-home pay, for each of the gross wages here. Add Federal Income Tax, State Income Tax, FICA, and Medicare to get total deductions. Subtract total deductions from the Gross Wages at the beginning of the line to get the Net Wages. You may use a calculator.

	Gross Wages	Federal Income Tax	State Income Tax	FICA	Medicare	Net Wages
1.	$87.50	$4.00	$3.50	$5.43	$1.27	$73.30
2.	$94.50	$5.00	$3.78	$5.86	$1.37	_____
3.	$198.00	$21.00	$7.92	$12.28	$2.87	_____
4.	$140.40	$13.00	$5.62	$8.70	$2.04	_____
5.	$98.80	$6.00	$3.95	$6.13	$1.43	_____
6.	$145.50	$13.00	$5.82	$9.02	$2.11	_____
7.	$96.00	$6.00	$3.84	$5.95	$1.39	_____
8.	$330.00	$40.00	$13.20	$20.46	$4.79	_____
9.	$136.75	$12.00	$5.47	$8.48	$1.98	_____
10.	$350.00	$45.00	$14.00	$21.70	$5.08	_____
11.	$119.90	$9.00	$4.80	$7.43	$1.74	_____
12.	$260.00	$30.00	$10.40	$16.12	$3.77	_____
13.	$123.65	$10.00	$4.95	$7.67	$1.79	_____
14.	$150.00	$13.00	$6.00	$9.30	$2.18	_____
15.	$205.25	$22.00	$8.21	$12.73	$2.98	_____
16.	$165.80	$16.00	$6.63	$10.28	$2.40	_____
17.	$187.15	$19.00	$7.49	$11.60	$2.71	_____
18.	$195.00	$20.00	$7.80	$12.09	$2.83	_____
19.	$210.50	$24.00	$8.42	$13.05	$3.05	_____
20.	$227.35	$25.00	$9.09	$14.10	$3.30	_____

What's the Bill?

Carla enjoyed her job at Runaway Sports Shop. She worked hard and was good at her job. She liked helping people and selling sporting goods. Below are some of the things Carla sold. Help her figure the total cost of the orders below. You may use a calculator. Write the total in the blank next to each order.

Total Cost

1. 2 baseballs, 1 baseball bat, 1 carryall bag $41.75
2. 1 dart game, 3 Frisbees, 2 packs of golf balls   _____
3. 2 tennis rackets, 2 racket covers, 2 cans of tennis balls   _____
4. 1 baseball glove, 1 pair of shoes, 3 baseballs   _____
5. 3 racket covers, 1 carryall bag, 3 pairs of socks   _____
6. 2 dart games, 1 Frisbee, 4 cans of tennis balls   _____
7. 2 baseball gloves, 4 baseballs, 1 pair of socks   _____
8. 4 packs of golf balls, 2 carryall bags, 4 pairs of socks   _____
9. 3 pairs of shoes, 6 pairs of socks, 1 baseball   _____
10. 2 Frisbees, 1 dart game, 3 cans of tennis balls   _____

Total Cost

11. 1 fishing pole, 1 net, 3 dozen fish hooks _____

12. 2 backpacks, 1 canteen, 2 sets of dishes _____

13. 2 compasses, 1 sleeping bag, 1 flashlight _____

14. 1 backpack, 2 flashlights, 4 batteries _____

15. 3 sets of dishes, 1 compass, 2 dozen fish hooks _____

16. 2 canteens, 2 sleeping bags, 3 batteries _____

17. 4 flashlights, 8 batteries, 2 nets _____

18. 5 backpacks, 5 canteens _____

19. 3 compasses, 3 flashlights _____

20. 3 fishing poles, 4 dozen fish hooks _____

21. 6 sets of dishes, 6 canteens _____

22. 1 sleeping bag, 2 flashlights, 2 batteries _____

23. 3 nets, 3 fishing poles, 5 dozen fish hooks _____

24. 4 backpacks, 4 sleeping bags _____

25. 2 fishing poles, 2 canteens, 2 compasses _____

Making Change

NAME _____

As a waiter, Steve had to know how to make change correctly. Here are some of his orders. Figure how much change Steve should give back for each order. Write the correct change in the blanks.

Order Costs	Money Paid	Amount of Change
1. $3.21		$ .04
2. $4.31		_____
3. $5.85		_____
4. $6.47		_____

Order Costs	Money Paid	Amount of Change
5. $3.97		_____
6. $7.44		_____
7. $9.20		_____
8. $12.55		_____
9. $8.20		_____
10. $14.10		_____

How Much Is There?

Mr. Swift, the store manager, asked Carla to find out how many tennis balls the store had altogether. Carla knew that there were 3 balls in each can. She knew that there were 12 cans in each case.

Use the picture to help Carla answer the questions below. Write your answers in the blanks.

1. How many cases of yellow tennis balls are there? _____4_____

2. How many cans of yellow tennis balls are there altogether? _____

3. How many yellow tennis balls are there altogether? _____

4. How many cases of green tennis balls are there? _____

5. How many cans of green tennis balls are there altogether? _____

6. How many green tennis balls are there altogether? _____

7. Each can of tennis balls sells for $2.79. What is the price of each ball? _____

8. What is the selling price of each case? _____

9. What is the total selling price of *all* the cases? _____

10. To make a profit, Mr. Swift sells the tennis balls for more than he paid for them. He paid $187.49 for all the cases. How much more is his selling price for all the cases? _____

Figuring the Cost

Runaway Sports Shop was selling tickets to a special baseball game. Figure the total cost of each group of tickets below. Write the total in the blanks.

1.

ADULT BASEBALL GAME $6.50 ADMIT 1   CHILD CHILD BASEBALL GAME $4.25 ADMIT 1

Total _$15.00_

2.

ADULT ADULT BASEBALL GAME $6.50 ADMIT 1   CHILD BASEBALL GAME $4.25 ADMIT 1

Total _____

3.

CHILD $ CHILD $ CHILD $ CHILD BASEBALL GAME $4.25 ADMIT 1

Total _____

4.

ADULT $ ADULT $ ADULT BASEBALL GAME $6.50 ADMIT 1

Total _____

5.

ADULT $ ADULT $ CHILD $ CHILD BASEBALL GAME $4.25 ADMIT 1

Total _____

6.

ADULT $ CHILD $ CHILD $ CHILD BASEBALL GAME $4.25 ADMIT 1

Total _____

7.

ADULT $ ADULT $ CHILD $ CHILD $ CHILD BASEBALL GAME $4.25 ADMIT 1

Total _____

8.

CHILD $ ADULT $ ADULT $ ADULT BASEBALL GAME $6.50 ADMIT 1

Total _____

9.

CHILD CHILD CHILD CHILD ADULT ADULT BASEBALL GAME $6.50 ADMIT 1

Total _____

10.

ADULT ADULT ADULT ADULT CHILD CHILD BASEBALL GAME $4.25 ADMIT 1

Total _____

28 twenty-eight

NAME _____

Start at the top left square of the maze. Follow the openings through the squares. Use a calculator. As you go, add the prices of the things Carla sold. Then fill in the blank for the total amount at the end of the maze.

SPORTS SHOP
Runaway

Baseball
$4.90 each
SOLD 4

Baseball hat
$6.19 each
SOLD 3

$49.95 each
SOLD 1

Golf balls
$1.20 each
SOLD 9

THIS WAY

Socks
$2.29/pair
SOLD 6 pairs

Shoes
$23.50/pair
SOLD 2 pairs

$2.99 each
SOLD 6

Frisbee
$5.69 each
SOLD 5

Fish hooks
$1.29/dozen
SOLD 8 dozen

Fishing net
$9.39
SOLD 2

$28.98 each
SOLD 2

THIS WAY

$13.98 each
SOLD 1

$21.99/pair
SOLD 1 pair

Fishing pole
$29.69 each
SOLD 1

Tent
$89.98 each

Compass
$6.97 each
SOLD 6

Canteen
$7.79 each
SOLD 3

$29.98/pair
SOLD 1 pair

$9.99 each
SOLD 2

Batteries
$1.32 each
SOLD 8

FREE

$18.00
SOLD 2

THIS WAY

FREE

Drawing for
ski trip

$22.79
SOLD 1

Flashlight
$5.25 each
SOLD 3

$24.79 each
SOLD 1

$32.19 each
SOLD 1

Tennis racket
cover
$5.95 each
SOLD 2

Tennis balls
$2.79/can
SOLD 7 cans

THIS WAY

Camping cups
$2.28 each
SOLD 4

TOTAL SALES

$ _____

These part-time employees at Runaway Sports Shop earn the same hourly wage. Figure the daily wages, weekly wages, and yearly wages for the six employees below. First, count and write the amount of money in the center of the wheel. Then work outward toward the rim. Follow the numbered steps one at a time, until you figure out what each employee earns in a year. As you work toward the rim, each answer is part of the next step. You may use a calculator.

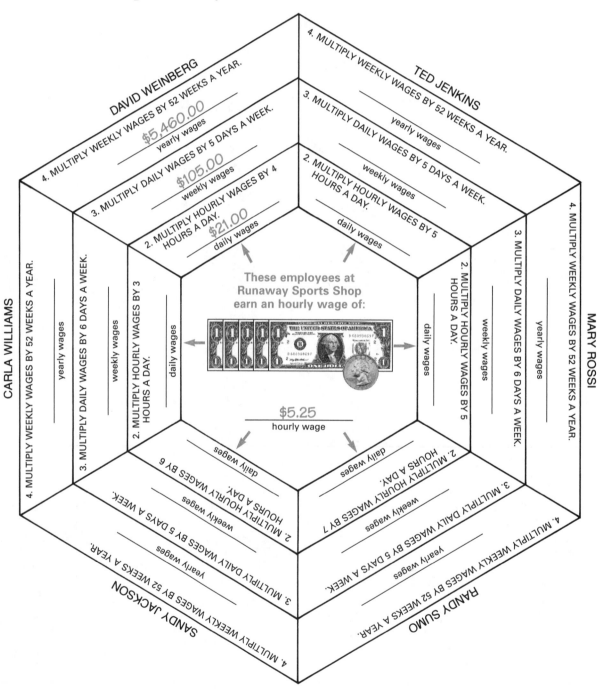

Half-Price Sale!

The Sandwich House was having a grand opening sale. For one day only, everything would be sold for half the regular price. Below are some of Steve's orders. To find the half price of each order, first figure the total, using the regular price. Then divide this amount by 2. Be sure to put the decimal point in the right place. Write your answers in the blanks.

The Sandwich House

Ham sandwich	$4.30	Soup	$1.75
Turkey sandwich	4.20	Salad	2.20
Fish sandwich	4.05	Milk, soft drinks	.85
Cheese sandwich	3.25	Coffee	.95
Chicken sandwich	4.15	Pie	1.90
Fruit plate	3.50	Ice cream	1.35

Order	Total	Half Price
1. 1 ham sandwich, 1 soup, 1 milk	$6.90	$3.45
2. 1 pie, 2 coffees	_____	_____
3. 1 cheese sandwich, 1 soft drink	_____	_____
4. 1 fruit plate, 1 milk, 1 ice cream	_____	_____
5. 1 chicken sandwich, 1 coffee	_____	_____
6. 1 soup, 1 soft drink	_____	_____
7. 1 fish sandwich, 1 milk, 1 pie	_____	_____

Order	Total	Half Price
8. 2 turkey sandwiches, 1 salad, 2 soft drinks	_____	_____
9. 1 fish sandwich, 1 chicken sandwich, 2 coffees	_____	_____
10. 1 cheese sandwich, 1 milk, 1 pie	_____	_____
11. 1 fruit plate, 1 soft drink, 1 ice cream	_____	_____
12. 2 ham sandwiches, 1 salad, 2 soft drinks	_____	_____
13. 2 chicken sandwiches, 2 soups, 2 milks	_____	_____
14. 3 fish sandwiches, 3 coffees	_____	_____
15. 1 ham sandwich, 1 chicken sandwich, 1 soup, 2 milks	_____	_____
16. 2 cheese sandwiches, 2 salads, 2 soft drinks	_____	_____
17. 4 turkey sandwiches, 2 milks, 2 coffees	_____	_____
18. 3 chicken sandwiches, 2 soups, 3 soft drinks	_____	_____
19. 2 fruit plates, 1 soup, 3 milks	_____	_____
20. 1 cheese sandwich, 1 ham sandwich, 3 coffees	_____	_____
21. 3 soups, 2 salads, 3 soft drinks	_____	_____
22. 5 ice creams, 5 coffees	_____	_____
23. 1 cheese sandwich, 1 fruit plate, 1 soup, 2 milks	_____	_____
24. 3 cheese sandwiches, 2 soups, 3 soft drinks	_____	_____
25. 4 ham sandwiches, 4 salads, 4 milks	_____	_____
26. 2 fruit plates, 3 soups, 3 soft drinks	_____	_____
27. 5 chicken sandwiches, 5 coffees, 2 ice creams	_____	_____
28. 3 fruit plates, 3 turkey sandwiches, 6 milks	_____	_____
29. 3 cheese sandwiches, 3 soups, 4 soft drinks	_____	_____
30. 4 pies, 3 ice creams, 7 coffees	_____	_____

Shopping Quiz

Both Steve and Carla needed to buy clothes for their new jobs. They saw this ad for Gant's Department Store in the newspaper. Read the ad. Then answer the questions on the next page.

GANT'S SUPER SALE
BUY ANY QUANTITY AT THESE SPECIAL SALE PRICES

Men's Socks

5 pairs for $9.95
(REGULAR PRICE—$11)

Any 2 Belts for $16.98

(REGULAR PRICE—$9 EACH)

Shirts

3 for $39.00
(REG.—$16 EACH)

Women's Socks

4 pairs for $10
(REGULAR PRICE—$3.50 A PAIR)

Save $12 When You Buy 2!

**Sweaters
2 for $44.00**

Men's and Women's Shoes

Any 2 pairs for $65
(REG.—$35 A PAIR)

SAVE $2 ON EVERY TIE!
Men's Ties

2 for $15

Women's Scarves

3 for $19.95
(REG.—$7 EACH)

1. What is the sale price of one pair of men's socks? $9.95 \div 5$ $1.99

   How much do four pairs cost? 1.99×4 $7.96

2. What is the sale price of one belt?   _____

   How much do three belts cost?   _____

3. What is the sale price of one shirt?   _____

   How much do two shirts cost?   _____

4. How much do four pairs of women's socks cost at the regular price?   _____

   How much money is saved by buying four pairs at the sale price?   _____

5. What is the sale price of one sweater?   _____

   How much more money does one sweater cost at the regular price?   _____

6. What is the sale price of one pair of shoes?   _____

   How much money is saved by buying two pairs of shoes at the sale price?   _____

7. What is the sale price of one tie?   _____

   What is the regular price of one tie?   _____

8. What is the sale price of one scarf?   _____

   How much do four scarves cost?   _____

9. At the sale, Steve bought three pairs of men's socks, two shirts, and three ties. How much money did he spend?   _____

   How much money did he save by buying the clothes on sale?   _____

   If Steve pays with three twenty-dollar bills, how much change will he get?   _____

10. At the sale, Carla bought two sweaters, one pair of shoes, and two scarves. How much money did she spend?   _____

    How much money did she save by buying these things on sale?   _____

    If Carla pays with six twenty-dollar bills, how much change will she get?   _____

NAME _____

Find the answers to these division problems. Be sure
to put the decimal point in the right place.

1.
```
     $ .93
  2)$1.86
    -18
     06
     -6
      0
```

2. 2)$32.64

3. 4)$39.00

4. 3)$5.67

5. 7)$14.07

6. 4)$27.76

7.
```
     $3.58
  3)$10.74
    -9
     17
    -15
     24
    -24
      0
```

8. 5)$43.25

9. 8)$68.56

10. 6)$7.32

11. 9)$36.36

12. 2)$7.28

13. 4)$14.92

14. 6)$44.76

15. 5)$36.75

16. 9)$24.93

17. 3)$13.02

18. 5)$11.40

19. 7)$23.94

20. 4)$7.16

21. 2)$7.70

22. 6)$58.92

23. 8)$79.68

24. 5)$97.15

The Wage Wheel

Figure the weekly, daily, and hourly wages for the six part-time employees of Gant's Department Store below. Start with the monthly wages for one employee. Follow the numbered steps for that employee outward toward the rim. Figure out the weekly, daily, and hourly wages for that person. As you work toward the rim, each answer is part of the next step. You may use a calculator.

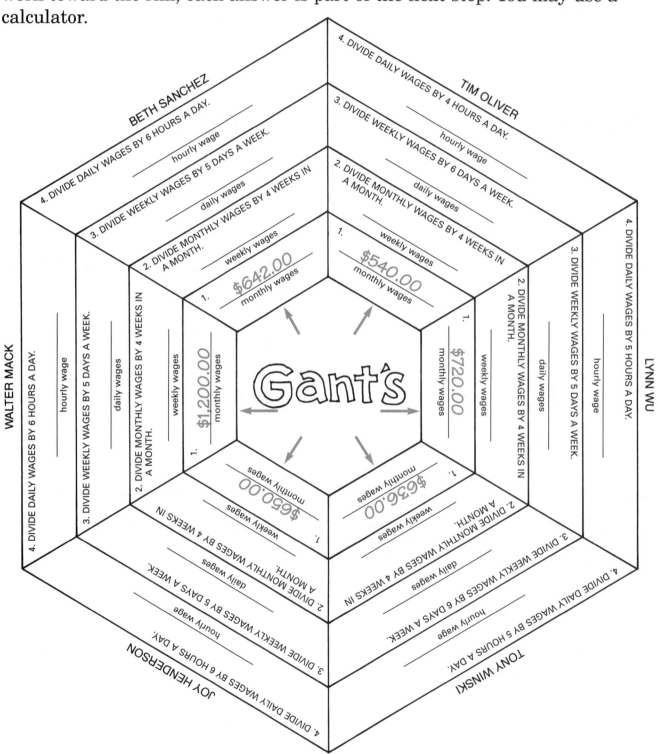

Bob Sommers had a full-time job at Franklin Florist. His job was to deliver flowers. One morning the owner, Ms. Franklin, asked Bob to find out how many miles the company station wagon got per gallon. He needed to figure out how many miles the station wagon could go on one gallon of gas.

FRANKLIN FLORIST

"I have a full tank of gas now," Bob said. "I'll keep track of how many miles I drive today. Then I'll buy more gas and see how many gallons I used. By dividing the number of miles driven by the number of gallons used, I'll know how many miles I get per gallon."

Before Bob started driving, he wrote down the mileage reading on the car's odometer.

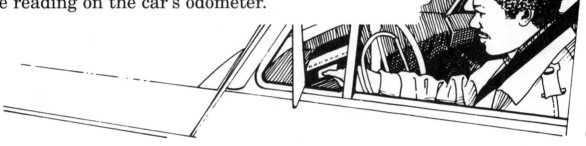

This was the mileage on the odometer at the start of the day.

3 7 8 2 5

This was the mileage on the odometer at the end of the day.

3 7 8 9 4

To find out how many miles he had gone, Bob subtracted his first mileage reading from the last one.

$$\begin{array}{r} 37894 \\ - \ 37825 \\ \hline 69 \end{array}$$ mileage at end of trip
mileage at start of trip
miles driven

Then Bob filled the tank again. It took 3 gallons. To find out how many miles he got per gallon, Bob divided the number of miles driven by the number of gallons of gas used.

gallons $3\overline{)69}$ 23 miles per gallon
miles driven

Now Bob knew how many miles the station wagon got per gallon. He knew he could drive about 23 miles on one gallon of gas.

Figure the gas mileage for the cars here. Write the number of miles each car was driven before filling up again. Then find the number of miles per gallon each car gets.

		Odometer at Start	Odometer at End	Miles Driven	Gallons Needed to Fill Tank Again	Miles per Gallon
	1.	41435	41580	145	5	29
	2.	48763	48889		6	
	3.	58354	58515		7	
	4.	16249	16409		10	
	5.	18716	18796		4	
	6.	32290	32395		3	
	7.	54178	54303		5	
	8.	42752	42860		6	
	9.	57279	57423		6	
	10.	27004	27300		8	
	11.	34148	34276		4	
	12.	23511	23731		10	
	13.	42632	42762		5	
	14.	71807	71959		4	
	15.	44427	44598		9	
	16.	26692	26794		6	
	17.	17886	18110		8	
	18.	40635	40873		7	
	19.	33833	33914		3	
	20.	12909	13119		10	

Decimal Division

One week, all Bob's driving was done on the highway. He knew that he probably got better gas mileage on the highway than in stop-and-go city driving. So he decided to find out for sure.

He checked the odometer when the tank was full. After a week of highway driving, he checked it again. By subtracting the first odometer reading from the second, Bob knew the car had been driven 369 miles.

First fill-up 3 8 2 7 6

Second fill-up 3 8 6 4 5

When the tank was filled again, Bob saw how many gallons he needed.

GALLONS: $14\frac{6}{10}$

To find the miles per gallon, Bob had to divide 369 by $14\frac{6}{10}$.

gallons $14\frac{6}{10}\overline{)369}$ miles driven

First he changed the $\frac{6}{10}$ to a decimal fraction. He knew that $\frac{6}{10}$ and .6 are just different ways of writing the same fraction.

six-tenths $= \frac{6}{10} = .6$

After he changed $\frac{6}{10}$ to a decimal fraction, the problem looked like this:

$14.6\overline{)369}$

Next, Bob moved the decimal point one place to the right in both numbers. He added two more zeros to the 369. Adding zeros to the right of the decimal point doesn't change the value of the number. Now he was ready to divide.

$14\,6.\overline{)369\,0,00}$

Bob worked out the problem to two decimal places. This means he stopped dividing when his answer had two numbers after the decimal point. He found that the station wagon got about 25.27 miles per gallon on the highway. This was over 2 miles per gallon more than in city driving.

$$
\begin{array}{r}
2\,5.27 \text{ miles per gallon} \\
14\,6.\overline{)369\,0.00} \\
-292 \\
\hline
77\,0 \\
-73\,0 \\
\hline
4\,0\,0 \\
-2\,9\,2 \\
\hline
1\,0\,80 \\
-1\,0\,22 \\
\hline
58
\end{array}
$$

Change these fractions to decimal fractions.

1. $12\frac{3}{10}$ _12.3_
2. $11\frac{7}{10}$ _____
3. $9\frac{6}{10}$ _____
4. $14\frac{2}{10}$ _____
5. $15\frac{9}{10}$ _____

6. $13\frac{4}{10}$ _____
7. $8\frac{8}{10}$ _____
8. $6\frac{1}{10}$ _____
9. $10\frac{5}{10}$ _____
10. $7\frac{7}{10}$ _____

11. $12\frac{8}{10}$ _____
12. $9\frac{3}{10}$ _____
13. $14\frac{7}{10}$ _____
14. $13\frac{8}{10}$ _____
15. $15\frac{2}{10}$ _____

Find the answers to these division problems. Remember to move the decimal point one place to the right before dividing. Work out each problem to two decimal places.

16.
```
        15.95
8 4.)134 0,0
   -84
    50 0
   -42 0
     80 0
    -75 6
     4 4 0
    -4 2 0
       2 0
```

17. $9.6\overline{)131}$

18. $8.5\overline{)107}$

19. $8.6\overline{)106}$

20. $5.8\overline{)120}$

21. $6.5\overline{)32}$

22. $12.1\overline{)156}$

23. $14.5\overline{)238}$

24. $11.7\overline{)177}$

25. $13.2\overline{)211}$

26. $15.4\overline{)223}$

27. $13.4\overline{)163}$

28. $10.8\overline{)150}$

29. $8.5\overline{)127}$

30. $13.9\overline{)189}$

31. $5.4\overline{)96}$

32. $10.6\overline{)230}$

33. $11.8\overline{)172}$

34. $12.9\overline{)224}$

35. $14.8\overline{)230}$

One day, Ms. Franklin asked Bob to drive to Columbia International Airport. He needed to pick up fresh flowers from Hawaii.

Bob got out a map and found that the airport was 162 miles away. He knew that the station wagon got about 25.3 miles per gallon of gas on the highway. How many gallons would the station wagon need to get to the airport? To find out, Bob divided the distance to the airport by the number of miles per gallon the car got.

$$
\begin{array}{r}
6.4 \\
25\underset{\curvearrowright}{.3\,)}\overline{162\underset{\curvearrowright}{\,0}.0} \\
-151\ 8 \\
\hline
10\ 2\ 0 \\
-10\ 1\ 2 \\
\hline
8
\end{array}
$$

6.4 **gallons needed**

miles per gallon · distance to the airport

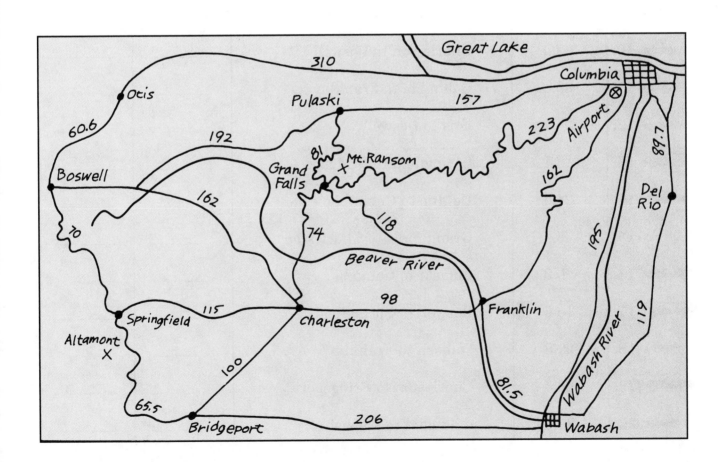

Use the map on page 41 to help you figure out how many gallons of gas each car would need to make these trips. Work out each problem to one decimal place.

	Miles per Gallon	Trip	Distance	Gallons Needed
1.	20.9	Franklin to Grand Falls	118	5.6
2.	28.2	Grand Falls to Columbia		
3.	34.8	Columbia to Otis		
4.	28.3	Wabash to Del Rio		
5.	17.8	Franklin to Charleston		
6.	19.3	Boswell to Pulaski		
7.	36.9	Springfield to Charleston		
8.	26.1	Grand Falls to Pulaski		
9.	21.9	Bridgeport to Wabash		
10.	32.4	Charleston to Boswell		
11.	36.8	Columbia to Franklin		
12.	24.1	Otis to Boswell		
13.	18.7	Springfield to Bridgeport		
14.	24.6	Del Rio to Columbia		
15.	35.2	Grand Falls to Charleston		
16.	20.9	Pulaski to Columbia		
17.	16.6	Boswell to Springfield		
18.	21.8	Wabash to Franklin		
19.	26.3	Charleston to Bridgeport		
20.	29.5	Columbia to Wabash		

NAME _____

One day, the Franklin Florist station wagon broke down. Ms. Franklin asked Bob to find out the cost for renting a small station wagon for the day.

Bob called two places that rented cars. He knew that he would drive about 75 miles. He used that figure to compare costs.

Call-a-Car charged $44.95 a day with free mileage. No matter how many miles Bob drove the car, it would still cost him $44.95.

$44.95 total cost (Call-a-Car)

Great Lake Rent-a-Car charged $24.00 a day and $.20 a mile. Bob multiplied $.20 by 75 miles to find the total mileage charge. Then he added this amount to the $24.00 daily charge to get the total cost.

```
   $ .20   cost per mile
 ×    75   miles
    100
    140
 $15.00   total mileage charge
```

```
 $15.00   total mileage charge
+ 24.00   daily charge
 $39.00   total cost
          (Great Lake Rent-a-Car)
```

Bob compared the total costs of each company. Great Lake Rent-a-Car had the lower total cost. To find out how much the car cost per mile, Bob divided the total cost by the number of miles he planned to drive. It cost about $.52 a mile to rent a car from Great Lake Rent-a-Car.

```
        $   .52   cost per mile
    75)$39.00
      − 37 5
        1 50
      − 1 50
           0
```

In each problem below, find out if Company A or Company B has the lower cost for renting a car. Use the total miles to be driven to compare costs. When you have found the lower cost for each problem, figure the cost per mile. Round your answer to two decimal places.

	Total Miles	Company A	Company B	Lower Total Cost	Lower Cost per Mile
1.	100	$35.00 a day Free mileage Total cost _$35.00_	$23.00 a day $.22 a mile Total cost _$45.00_	Company _A_ $ _$35.00_	$ _.35_
2.	75.5	$21.95 a day $.22 a mile Total cost _____	$39.95 a day Free mileage Total cost _____	Company _____ $ _____	$ _____
3.	54.2	$47.00 a day Free mileage Total cost _____	$22.77 a day $.25 a mile Total cost _____	Company _____ $ _____	$ _____
4.	38.6	$25.95 a day Free mileage Total cost _____	$22.50 a day $.25 a mile Total cost _____	Company _____ $ _____	$ _____
5.	71.5	$22.50 a day $.26 a mile Total cost _____	$36.25 a day Free mileage Total cost _____	Company _____ $ _____	$ _____
6.	98.3	$24.95 a day $.20 a mile Total cost _____	$36.50 a day Free mileage Total cost _____	Company _____ $ _____	$ _____
7.	45.5	$24.75 a day $.24 a mile Total cost _____	$42.95 a day Free mileage Total cost _____	Company _____ $ _____	$ _____
8.	30.8	$21.50 a day $.30 a mile Total cost _____	$28.75 a day Free mileage Total cost _____	Company _____ $ _____	$ _____
9.	66.5	$22.00 a day $.26 a mile Total cost _____	$41.95 a day Free mileage Total cost _____	Company _____ $ _____	$ _____
10.	120	$21.25 a day $.23 a mile Total cost _____	$41.00 a day Free mileage Total cost _____	Company _____ $ _____	$ _____

NAME _____

The Franklin Florist station wagon needed two new tires. Ms. Franklin looked through the newspaper to see which store had the lowest price. Here are three of the ads she saw in the paper.

1. How much does one tire cost at Abbott's Garage? _____

   How much does one tire cost at J&G Auto? _____

2. At which store would Ms. Franklin get the lowest price if she wanted to buy only one tire? _____

3. How much do two tires cost at Wheelmart? _____

   How much do two tires cost at J&G Auto? _____

4. Which store has the lowest price for two tires? _____

5. If Ms. Franklin buys two tires at J&G Auto, how much will she save by buying them on sale? _____

Take a Trip

Find out how fast each car is driven for the distances shown below. Speed is measured in miles per hour. To figure miles per hour, divide the number of miles driven by the number of hours.

Example:

$$16\overline{)480}.$$

with quotient 30, and -480, remainder 00.

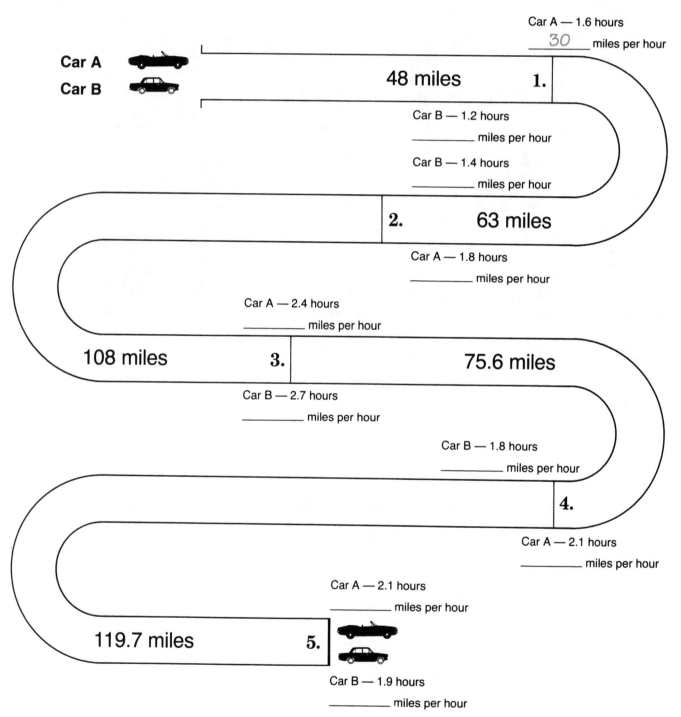

Car A — 1.6 hours

_____30_____ miles per hour

Car A

Car B

48 miles   **1.**

Car B — 1.2 hours

_____ miles per hour

Car B — 1.4 hours

_____ miles per hour

2.   63 miles

Car A — 1.8 hours

_____ miles per hour

Car A — 2.4 hours

_____ miles per hour

108 miles   **3.**   **75.6 miles**

Car B — 2.7 hours

_____ miles per hour

Car B — 1.8 hours

_____ miles per hour

4.

Car A — 2.1 hours

_____ miles per hour

Car A — 2.1 hours

_____ miles per hour

119.7 miles   5.

Car B — 1.9 hours

_____ miles per hour

6. Which car finished the trip first? _____

A Checking Account

Soon after Carla Williams started working at Runaway Sports Shop, she opened a checking account at the bank. She knew that having a checking account was a good way to handle her money.

Here are some of the reasons a checking account is good to have.

- You don't have to carry a lot of money with you to pay for things. In many stores, you can write a check to pay for what you buy.
- Checks are a safe and easy way to pay bills by mail. No one can cash a check except the person, store, or company to whom it is made out. Money sent by mail can get lost or stolen.
- When you write a check, there is a record that you paid for what you bought. A copy of the canceled check can be your written record.

Writing a check to pay for something is like paying cash for it. But the money is in your checking account and not in your pocket. You must have enough money in your checking account to cover the check. Your bank will pay the person, store, or company you name on the check with the money in your account.

After your bank pays the money for each check you write, the check is *canceled*. A canceled check cannot be used again. At the end of the month, your bank sends you a *statement* that lists all your canceled checks. If you need a copy of a canceled check, you can contact your bank. The copy will be your record that you paid for the things you bought.

Answer YES or NO to these questions.

1. Can Carla write a check to pay for something in a store? _____

2. Are canceled checks a record that you paid for what you bought? _____

3. Can a canceled check be used again? _____

4. Should Carla have enough money in her account to cover the

checks she writes? _____

Complete each sentence by drawing a line from the left
to the best ending on the right.

carry a lot of money with her.

5. Carla opened a checking account
so she could

write checks.

send the money.

6. A good way to pay bills by
mail is to

send a check.

paying cash for it.

7. Writing a check to pay for
something is like

saving money to pay for it.

paid for the thing you bought.

8. A copy of a canceled check
shows that you

don't have any money in your account.

Understanding Checks

Carla bought two Frisbees from Runaway Sports Shop.
Here is the check she wrote to pay for them.

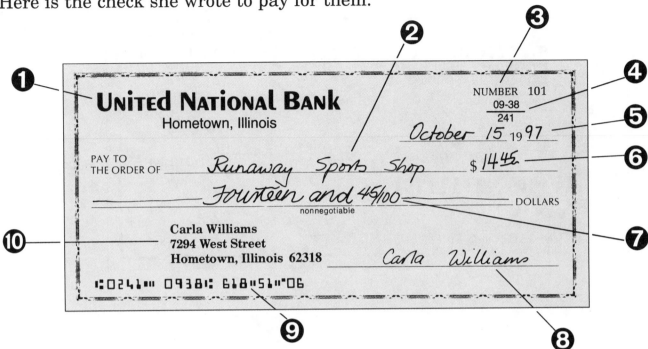

Here are the things that are on this check.

❶   The name of the bank where Carla has her checking account.

❷   The name of the company to which Carla wrote the check. Runaway
Sports Shop will cash this check to get its money.

❸   The number of the check. The checks are numbered in order, so the next
check Carla writes will be Number 102.

❹   The bank number. Every bank has its own number above the line.
(A government bank number is below the line.)

❺   The date. Carla wrote this check on October 15.

❻   The amount of the check written in numbers. Carla wrote this check
for $14.45.

❼   The dollar amount of the check spelled out in words.

❽   Carla's signature. Carla must sign her name on the check before her
bank will cash it and pay Runaway Sports Shop.

❾   Carla's account number at the bank.

❿   Carla's name and address. This shows that the check belongs to Carla.

Here is another check. Study it and answer the
questions below.

```
SYLVIA KREBS                          Number  214
2369 HURON STREET                            13-02
BERWYN, ILLINOIS 62300                       ─────
                                             1074
                              August 24 19 97

Pay to the Order of  Martin Stern      $ 27 49

──────────  Twenty-seven and 49/100  ────── DOLLARS
                     nonnegotiable
GREENBRIER
BANK  BERWYN, ILLINOIS        Sylvia Krebs

⑈1074⑈ 1302⑈ 85⑈9361⑈0
```

1. Who wrote this check? _____

2. At what bank does Sylvia Krebs have her checking account? _____

   _____

3. Where does Sylvia Krebs live? _____

   _____

4. To whom did Sylvia Krebs make out this check? _____

   _____

5. What is the number of this check? _____

6. On what date was this check written? _____

7. What is the amount of this check? _____

8. In how many places on the check is the amount shown? _____

9. What is the bank number? _____

When Carla opened her checking account, the bank gave her a list of rules for writing checks. These rules showed her the correct way to write checks.

RULES FOR WRITING CHECKS

1. Always use a pen to write a check. Never write a check with a pencil.
2. Never change figures on a check. If you make a mistake, tear up the check and write a new one.
3. Fill all the blanks on the check with words, numbers, or lines.
4. Be sure to use the correct date.
5. Never write a check for more than the amount in your checking account.
6. If a check is lost or stolen, ask the bank to stop payment on it.

Carla also learned how to write the amount on the check both in figures and in words.

Write the amount in numbers close to the dollar sign ($) on the check. On the next line, write the amount of dollars in words. Then write *and*. Then write the amount of cents in hundredths.

United National Bank
Hometown, Illinois

NUMBER 103
09-38
241

October 20, 1997

PAY TO THE ORDER OF _Gant's Department Store_ $ 74 30

———————— Seventy-four and 30/100 ———————— DOLLARS
nonnegotiable

Carla Williams
7294 West Street
Hometown, Illinois 62318

Carla Williams

⑆0241⑆ 0938⑆ 618⑈51⑈06

The amount of the next check Carla wrote was $9.67.

She wrote the amount in figures like this. $ _____ 9⁶⁷ _____

She wrote the amount in words like this. ___Nine and ⁶⁷⁄₁₀₀_____ DOLLARS

Write these amounts for the checks in words.

	Amount	Words	
1.	$8.52	Eight and ⁵²⁄₁₀₀	DOLLARS
2.	$115.69	One Hundred Fifteen and ⁶⁹⁄₁₀₀	DOLLARS
3.	$71.80		DOLLARS
4.	$16.97		DOLLARS
5.	$10.22		DOLLARS
6.	$49.51		DOLLARS
7.	$20.82		DOLLARS
8.	$339.17		DOLLARS
9.	$25.12		DOLLARS
10.	$212.39		DOLLARS
11.	$31.40		DOLLARS
12.	$52.33		DOLLARS
13.	$164.10		DOLLARS
14.	$19.18		DOLLARS
15.	$97.05		DOLLARS

Writing Checks

Carla bought new clothes at Gant's Department Store.
She wrote this check to pay for the clothes.

UNITED NATIONAL BANK
Hometown, Illinois

NUMBER 103
09-38
————
241

October 20 19 97 ____

PAY TO
THE ORDER OF *Gant's Department Store* $ 74 30

———————— *Seventy-four and* 30/100 ———————— DOLLARS
                                    nonnegotiable

Carla Williams
7294 West Street
Hometown, Illinois 62318

Carla Williams

⑊0241⑊ 0938⑊ 618⑊51⑊06

Study the check that Carla wrote. Then make out the
checks on this page and the next for the amounts
shown. Use today's date and sign your own name.

1. To Jennifer Shikamura for $32.28.

River Valley Bank
River Valley, Ohio

Number
144

01-16
————
815

_____ 19 ____

Pay to
the Order of _____ $ _____

_____ Dollars
                  nonnegotiable

_____

⑊0815 ⑊ 0116⑊ 49 378⑊01⑊

2. To Kaplan's Electronics for $116.59.

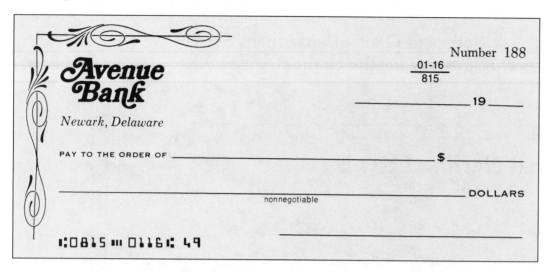

3. To Entropy Power Company for $19.07.

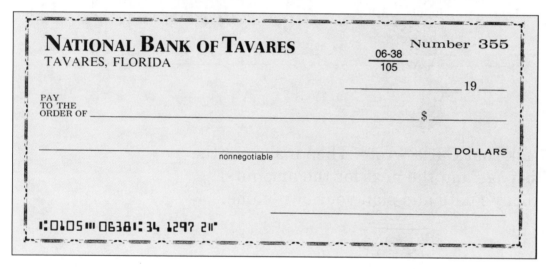

4. To Noyes Music Shop for $17.00.

Writing Checks

Make out the checks here for the amounts shown. Use today's date and sign your own name.

1. To Hammer Hardware for $21.50.

PLAINS BANK
PUTNEY, VERMONT

Number 299
13-02
————
1074

_____ 19 _____

PAY TO
THE ORDER OF _____ $ _____

_____ DOLLARS
nonnegotiable

_____

⑈1074⑈ 1302⑈ 85⑈9361⑈0

2. To Cyclops TV Repair for $43.07.

NATIONAL BANK *MERLIN, OREGON*
& TRUST COMPANY

NUMBER
257
10-74
————
1302

_____ 19 _____

PAY TO
THE ORDER OF _____ $ _____

_____ DOLLARS
nonnegotiable

_____

⑈1302⑈ 1074⑈ 85⑈9361⑈0

3. To Grand Garage for $98.13.

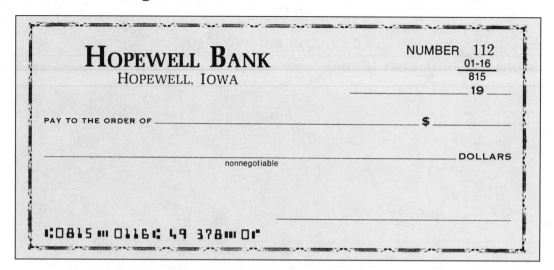

4. To Baron Flying School for $156.50.

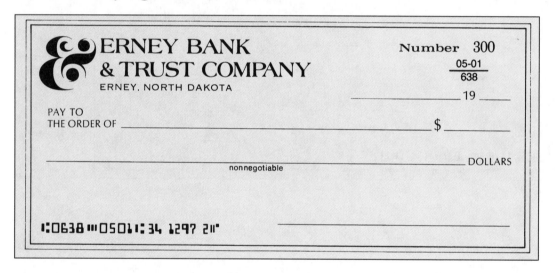

5. To Penelope Weaving, Inc. for $14.40.

The Checkbook Register

Carla started her checking account by putting $200.00 in the bank. Any money that is put into a bank account is called a *deposit*. This deposit was also her *balance*—the total amount of money she had in her account. Carla made a record of the deposit in her checkbook register. She used the checkbook register to keep a record of her deposits and a record of the checks she wrote.

Here is how Carla recorded her first deposit in her checkbook register.

CHECK NO.	DATE	CHECKS ISSUED TO OR DESCRIPTION OF DEPOSIT	AMOUNT OF CHECK	✔	AMOUNT OF DEPOSIT	BALANCE	
–	10/7	deposit			200 | 00	200	00

The first check Carla wrote was for $14.45. She wrote this check to Runaway Sports Shop to pay for two Frisbees. Carla made a record of the check in her checkbook register. Here are the things she recorded:

- the number of the check
- the date she wrote the check
- to whom she wrote the check
- the reason for the check
- the amount of the check
- the new balance in the account

Here is how Carla recorded her check to Runaway Sports Shop. To find the new balance, Carla subtracted the amount of the check from the old balance.

CHECK NO.	DATE	CHECKS ISSUED TO OR DESCRIPTION OF DEPOSIT	AMOUNT OF CHECK	✔	AMOUNT OF DEPOSIT	BALANCE	
–	10/7	deposit			200 | 00	200	00
101	10/15	Runaway Sports Shop (Frisbees)	14 | 45			185	55

The second check Carla wrote was for $9.67. Here is how she recorded the check in her checkbook register.

CHECK NO.	DATE	CHECKS ISSUED TO OR DESCRIPTION OF DEPOSIT	AMOUNT OF CHECK		✔	AMOUNT OF DEPOSIT		BALANCE	
—	10/7	deposit				200	00	200	00
101	10/15	Runaway Sports Shop (Frisbees)	14	45				185	55
102	10/18	Noyes Music Shop (cassette tape)	9	67				175	88

Carla wrote check Number 103, shown below, to pay for new clothes. Make a record of this check in Carla's checkbook register above. To find the new balance, subtract the amount of the check from the old balance.

UNITED NATIONAL BANK
Hometown, Illinois

NUMBER 103
09-38
241

October 20 19 97

PAY TO THE ORDER OF   Gant's Department Store $ 74 30

Seventy-four and 30/100 ——————— DOLLARS

nonnegotiable

Carla Williams
7294 West Street
Hometown, Illinois 62318

Carla Williams

⑆0241⑆ 0938⑈ 618 51 06

Carla wrote check Number 104 on October 28. She wrote the check to the *Good News Paper* to pay for her newspaper. The amount of the check was $6.25. Make a record of this check in her checkbook register above. Then figure the new balance.

Balancing the Register

Complete this checkbook register. Figure the new balance for each check written and each deposit made. Remember to *subtract* checks and *add* deposits. You may use a calculator to complete the register.

CHECK NO.	DATE	CHECKS ISSUED TO OR DESCRIPTION OF DEPOSIT	AMOUNT OF CHECK	✔	AMOUNT OF DEPOSIT	BALANCE 427 35
201	4/12	Graham Telephone (telephone)	16 24			
202	4/14	IRS (taxes)	58 17			
203	4/14	Maze Dept. Store (clothes)	55 98			
204	4/15	Entropy Power Co. (electric bill)	30 25			
–	4/15	deposit			400 00	
205	4/22	Sundial Jewelers (watch repair)	25 00			
206	4/25	Best Supermarket (groceries)	51 08			
207	4/27	Poore Circulation Co. (magazine)	14 50			
–	4/28	deposit			300 00	
208	5/1	Hillcrest Apartments (rent)	575 00			
209	5/1	Eastside Savings & Loan (savings)	150 00			
210	5/8	OPEC Oil (gasoline)	47 25			
211	5/8	Sparkle Cleaners (dry cleaning)	8 53			
212	5/10	Franklin Drugstore (vitamins)	6 76			

Complete this checkbook register. Figure the new
balance for each check written and each deposit made.
Remember to *subtract* checks and *add* deposits. You
may use a calculator to complete the register.

CHECK NO.	DATE	CHECKS ISSUED TO OR DESCRIPTION OF DEPOSIT	AMOUNT OF CHECK		✔	AMOUNT OF DEPOSIT		BALANCE 606	71
578	1/26	Fiesta Foods (groceries)	69	89					
579	1/27	Ernie's Garage (oil change)	15	95					
580	1/27	Dr. Yankard (dentist bill)	42	50					
—	1/31	deposit				289	75		
581	2/1	Crown Colony (rent)	545	00					
582	2/5	Longlife Insurance (insurance)	37	85					
583	2/10	Hoopla Theater (tickets)	26	50					
584	2/14	Franklin Florist (flowers)	21	95					
585	2/14	The White Horse (dinner)	32	75					
—	2/15	deposit				425	00		
586	2/18	Great Bank (credit card payment)	78	18					
587	2/18	Ford Motors (car payment)	196	95					
588	2/20	Fiesta Foods (groceries)	25	98					
—	2/28	deposit				375	00		

NAME _____

Make a record of these checks and add the deposit in the checkbook register below. Write in all the facts shown. Figure the new balance after each check or deposit. The first one has been done for you.

1. Check Number 105. December 1. To Snow Plow, Inc. For snow blowing. $20.00.

2. Check Number 106. December 3. To Tip Toe Shoes. For boots. $64.79.

3. Check Number 107. December 8. To Franklin Electric. For electricity bill. $37.23.

4. Check Number 108. December 12. To Super Oil Company. For gas. $59.08.

5. Deposit. December 15. $315.00.

6. Check Number 109. December 16. To Noel Evergreens. For Christmas tree. $34.50.

7. Check Number 110. December 20. To Fiesta Foods. For groceries. $73.86.

8. Check Number 111. December 23. To United Charge-It-All. For credit card. $229.99.

CHECK NO.	DATE	CHECKS ISSUED TO OR DESCRIPTION OF DEPOSIT	AMOUNT OF CHECK		✔	AMOUNT OF DEPOSIT		BALANCE	
								231	07
105	12/1	Snow Plow, Inc. (snow blowing)	20	00				211	07

Make a record of these checks and deposits in the checkbook register below. Write in all the facts shown. Figure the new balance after each check or deposit.

1. Check Number 238. July 9. To Dr. Murphy. For checkup. $50.00.

2. Deposit. July 11. $465.71.

3. Check Number 239. July 12. To North Savings & Loan. For savings. $100.00.

4. Check Number 240. July 13. To Trust Insurance. For car insurance. $162.60.

5. Check Number 241. July 15. To Handy Hardware. For paint. $47.85.

6. Check Number 242. July 20. To *Good News Paper.* For newspapers. $6.25.

7. Deposit. July 25. $45.00.

8. Check Number 243. July 30. To Lender's Bank. For car payment. $210.15.

CHECK NO.	DATE	CHECKS ISSUED TO OR DESCRIPTION OF DEPOSIT	AMOUNT OF CHECK	✔	AMOUNT OF DEPOSIT	BALANCE 84 30	

Deposit Slips

Carla filled out a deposit slip each time she put money in her checking account. Each deposit slip had her name, address, and account number printed on it.

On October 31, Carla deposited the cash and checks shown below. Here is how she filled out her deposit slip.

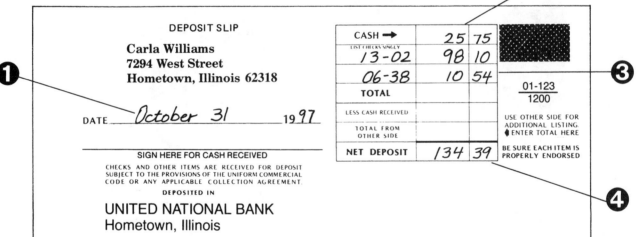

❶ She wrote the date she made the deposit.

❷ She wrote the total amount of cash here.

❸ She listed her checks separately here. On the left, she wrote the bank number (only the number above the line) of each check she deposited. Then she wrote the amount of each check.

❹ She added the amounts of the cash and the checks to get her total deposit.

Steve Pollard deposited the checks shown below, but he didn't put the whole amount into his account. Instead, he wanted part of the amount back in cash.

To get the cash back, he had to sign his name on the deposit slip. He also had to write the amount he wanted, $10.00, in the space marked *less cash received*. He then subtracted $10.00 from the total of the checks.

Fill in Steve's deposit slip below with the amounts of money shown on the checks. Use today's date. Remember to list each check separately. Add these amounts to get the *total*. Then subtract the $10.00 to get the *net deposit*—the amount that would go into Steve's account.

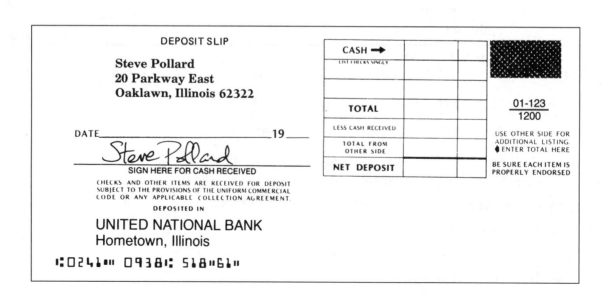

Fill out the deposit slip below for the amounts of money shown here. Use today's date. Remember to list each check separately. Then add to find the total amount of the deposit.

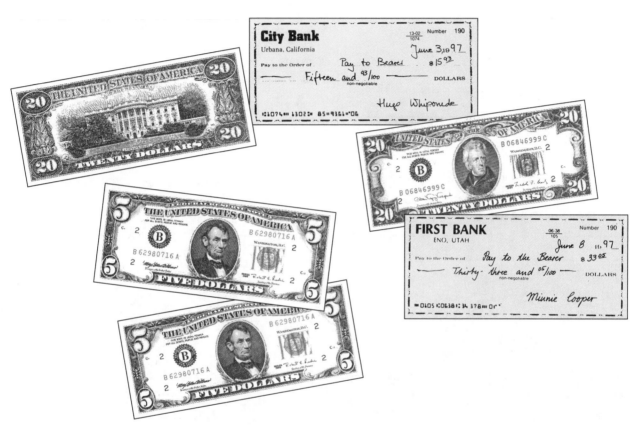

1.

DEPOSIT SLIP		CASH ➡			
		LIST CHECKS SINGLY			
					01-123 / 1200
		TOTAL			
DATE_____ 19___		LESS CASH RECEIVED			USE OTHER SIDE FOR ADDITIONAL LISTING. ◆ ENTER TOTAL HERE
		TOTAL FROM OTHER SIDE			
SIGN HERE FOR CASH RECEIVED		**NET DEPOSIT**			BE SURE EACH ITEM IS PROPERLY ENDORSED

CHECKS AND OTHER ITEMS ARE RECEIVED FOR DEPOSIT SUBJECT TO THE PROVISIONS OF THE UNIFORM COMMERCIAL CODE OR ANY APPLICABLE COLLECTION AGREEMENT.
DEPOSITED IN
UNITED NATIONAL BANK
Hometown, Illinois

⑆0241⑈ 0938⑈ 618″51″06

2.

DEPOSIT SLIP

CASH ➡
LIST CHECKS SINGLY

TOTAL

DATE_____ 19 ___

LESS CASH RECEIVED

TOTAL FROM
OTHER SIDE

01-123
1200

USE OTHER SIDE FOR
ADDITIONAL LISTING.
◆ ENTER TOTAL HERE

SIGN HERE FOR CASH RECEIVED

NET DEPOSIT

BE SURE EACH ITEM IS
PROPERLY ENDORSED

CHECKS AND OTHER ITEMS ARE RECEIVED FOR DEPOSIT
SUBJECT TO THE PROVISIONS OF THE UNIFORM COMMERCIAL
CODE OR ANY APPLICABLE COLLECTION AGREEMENT.
DEPOSITED IN

UNITED NATIONAL BANK
Hometown, Illinois

⑆0241⑆ 0938⑈ 618⑈51⑈06

3.

DEPOSIT SLIP

CASH ➡
LIST CHECKS SINGLY

TOTAL

DATE_____ 19 ___

LESS CASH RECEIVED

TOTAL FROM
OTHER SIDE

01-123
1200

USE OTHER SIDE FOR
ADDITIONAL LISTING.
◆ ENTER TOTAL HERE

SIGN HERE FOR CASH RECEIVED

NET DEPOSIT

BE SURE EACH ITEM IS
PROPERLY ENDORSED

CHECKS AND OTHER ITEMS ARE RECEIVED FOR DEPOSIT
SUBJECT TO THE PROVISIONS OF THE UNIFORM COMMERCIAL
CODE OR ANY APPLICABLE COLLECTION AGREEMENT.
DEPOSITED IN

UNITED NATIONAL BANK
Hometown, Illinois

⑆0241⑆ 0938⑈ 618⑈51⑈06

A Savings Account

There are several ways your money can earn more money when saving with a bank. There are Individual Retirement Accounts (IRA's), Certificates of Deposit (CD's), Money Fund Plus accounts, and Savings Accounts. These are the most commonly used methods of saving money.

Soon after Steve Pollard started working at The Sandwich House, he thought about saving money. He decided to open a savings account at Farmers First Bank.

Each time Steve wanted to put money into his account, he had to fill out a deposit slip. On November 21, Steve deposited the cash and checks shown below. Here is how he filled out his deposit slip.

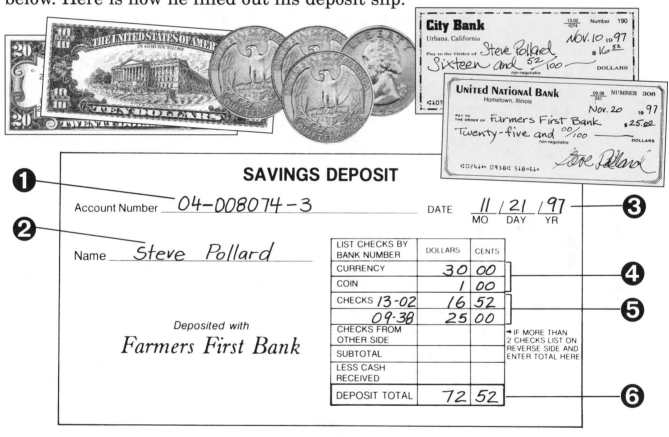

❶ He wrote his savings account number here.

❷ He printed his name here.

❸ He wrote the date he made the deposit.

❹ He listed the amount of bills and coins separately here.

❺ He listed the bank number and the amount of each check here.

❻ He added the amounts of the cash and the checks to get his total deposit.

Fill out the deposit slips below with the amounts of
money shown. Use today's date and print your own
name.

1.

SAVINGS DEPOSIT

Account Number ___07- 100099-9___   DATE ___/___/___
                                         MO DAY YR

Name _____

LIST CHECKS BY BANK NUMBER	DOLLARS	CENTS
CURRENCY		
COIN		
CHECKS		
CHECKS FROM OTHER SIDE		
SUBTOTAL		
LESS CASH RECEIVED		
DEPOSIT TOTAL		

◄ IF MORE THAN 2 CHECKS LIST ON REVERSE SIDE AND ENTER TOTAL HERE

Deposited with
Farmers First Bank

2.

SAVINGS DEPOSIT

Account Number ___01 - 50666 - 8___   DATE ___/___/___
                                           MO DAY YR

Name _____

LIST CHECKS BY BANK NUMBER	DOLLARS	CENTS
CURRENCY		
COIN		
CHECKS		
CHECKS FROM OTHER SIDE		
SUBTOTAL		
LESS CASH RECEIVED		
DEPOSIT TOTAL		

◄ IF MORE THAN 2 CHECKS LIST ON REVERSE SIDE AND ENTER TOTAL HERE

Deposited with
Farmers First Bank

When Steve opened his savings account, the bank gave him a passbook. The passbook showed how much money Steve had in his account. Each time Steve put money into his account, the bank teller recorded the deposit in Steve's passbook. Sometimes Steve took some money out of his account. This is called making a *withdrawal*. Each time Steve made a withdrawal, the teller recorded it in Steve's passbook.

The bank paid Steve money for keeping his savings there. This money is called *interest*. The amount of interest Steve earned on his savings was also shown in his passbook. The last column in the passbook showed the balance in the account after each deposit or withdrawal.

DATE	WITHDRAWAL	DEPOSIT	INTEREST	BALANCE
11/21		72.52		72.52
11/30		25.00	.12	97.64
12/15	35.00			62.64
12/31	40.00		.31	22.95
1/13		30.00		52.95
1/31		25.00	.17	78.12

Here is how Steve's passbook looked after three months. Study the passbook and answer the questions below.

1. How much money did Steve have in his account after making his second deposit? _____

2. On December 31, what was Steve's balance? _____

3. How much did Steve withdraw *altogether* from his account? _____

4. How much did Steve deposit *altogether* in his account? _____

5. How much interest did Steve earn on his savings? _____

Bob Sommers also had a savings account at Farmers First Bank. Here are the entries for his account for four months.

DATE	ENTRY	AMOUNT
3/2	Deposit	38.50
3/20	Deposit	25.00
3/30	Deposit	45.00
3/30	Interest	.12
4/6	Withdrawal	35.50
4/21	Deposit	23.75

DATE	ENTRY	AMOUNT
5/4	Deposit	30.00
5/25	Withdrawal	25.00
5/31	Interest	1.17
6/1	Deposit	36.50
6/15	Deposit	23.50
6/29	Withdrawal	50.00

Write each entry in the correct column of Bob's passbook. Remember to figure the new balance after each entry.

DATE	WITHDRAWAL	DEPOSIT	INTEREST	BALANCE
3/2		38.50		38.50

On June 29, what was Bob's balance? _____

Write each of these entries in the correct column of the passbook below. Figure the new balance after each entry.

DATE	ENTRY	AMOUNT
6/1	Deposit	50.00
6/15	Deposit	38.50
7/6	Withdrawal	20.00
7/18	Deposit	52.25
7/31	Interest	.85
8/10	Deposit	46.75
8/18	Deposit	15.00
8/27	Withdrawal	35.00

DATE	ENTRY	AMOUNT
9/7	Deposit	55.00
9/21	Deposit	32.75
9/28	Interest	1.60
10/1	Deposit	48.50
10/12	Withdrawal	50.00
10/16	Deposit	25.00
11/9	Withdrawal	37.00
11/23	Deposit	20.00

DATE	WITHDRAWAL	DEPOSIT	INTEREST	BALANCE
6/1		50.00		50.00

On November 23, what was the balance in this account? _____

Figure each person's balance by adding deposits and interest and by subtracting withdrawals. Start with the deposit in the center of the wheel. Work outward toward the rim, following the numbered steps for one person at a time, until you figure out each person's balance. As you work toward the rim, each answer is part of the next problem. You may use a calculator.

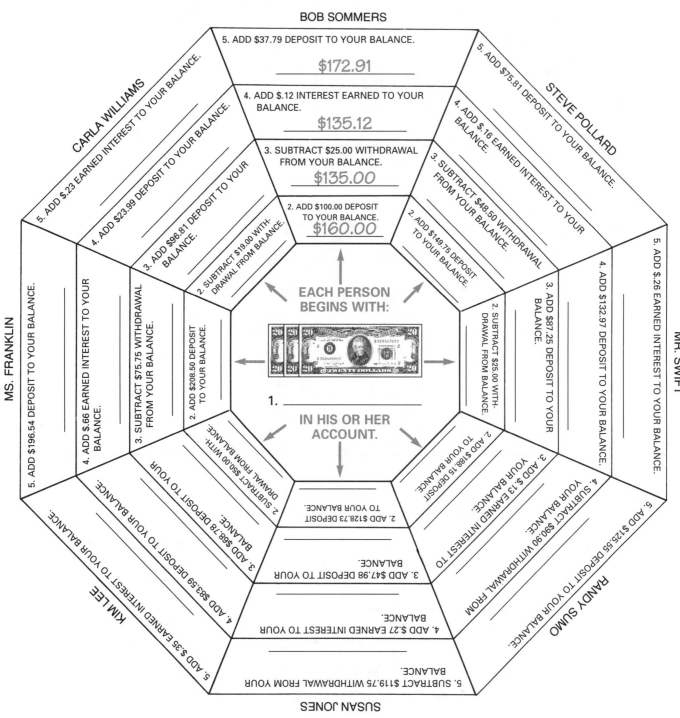

NAME _____

Sometimes Carla wanted to go to the bank in the evening or on the weekend. But her bank wasn't open during these times. Carla discovered that her bank had an *automated teller machine (ATM)*. An ATM is a computer-operated machine that does bank *transactions*—usually deposits and withdrawals. The ATM at Carla's bank operated every day from six in the morning until midnight. Some ATMs are open 24 hours a day.

Here are some reasons for using an ATM.

- You can get money from your account, even when the bank is closed.
- The lines at the teller machines are often shorter than inside the bank.
- At some stores and gas stations, you can use your ATM card instead of writing a check. The amount is subtracted from your account.

Carla filled out an application for an ATM card. She soon got the card in the mail. The card had a number printed on the front. It also came with a four-digit code that was not on the card. This code was for Carla to use when starting a transaction. No one but Carla would know the code. This way, only Carla could use her card to take money from her account.

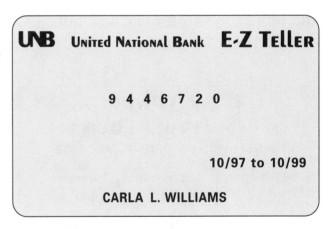

Here are some things to remember about using an ATM card.

- You can only withdraw money that you have in your account.
- You should never deposit cash.
- Most banks have a limit on the amount you can withdraw each day.
- Some banks may charge you a fee, too.
- If you must go to an ATM at night, bring a friend. Make sure the ATM is well lighted and in a populated area.

One day Carla went to the bank. She wanted to take some money from her checking account. The line inside the bank was long, so she decided to use the ATM. She started the transaction by putting her ATM card into the slot on the teller machine. Then she pressed the number buttons to enter her personal 4-digit code.

Instructions appeared on the screen, telling Carla which buttons to push for each step. The buttons she pushed told the machine how much money she wanted, and from which of her accounts she wanted to take it. The money came out through another slot on the machine. Carla took the money, then pushed a button to show that she was finished. Her card was returned, and she received a record of her transaction.

❶E-Z Teller
United National Bank
TRANSACTION RECORD—PLEASE SAVE

ATM Number	Card Number	❹ Transaction
❷ 0838	❸ 9446720	Withdrawal

❺ Amount	Date	❻ Time
$40.00	12/22/97	1:20 p.m.

❼ Account	Location	New Balance
Checking #618-51-06	Hometown Shopping ❽ Center	❾ $308.56

THANK YOU

Transaction Records

These are the items that appeared on Carla's transaction record.

❶ *E-Z Teller.* This is the name United National Bank uses for its automated teller machines.

❷ *The ATM number.* Each United National Bank has its own number.

❸ *The number on Carla's ATM card.* This number is different from Carla's account number, and it's different from her four-digit code.

❹ *The type of transaction.* Carla made a withdrawal from her account.

❺ *The amount of money Carla took out.* Each bank has a limit on the amount a person can take out each day. The limit at Carla's bank is $200.00.

❻ *The date and time* that the transaction took place.

❼ *Carla's checking account number.*

❽ *The place the transaction was made.* This United National Bank is in the Hometown Shopping Center.

❾ *Carla's balance.* This is the amount in her account *after* she took out the $40.00.

Using the transaction record, Carla made a record of her withdrawal in her checkbook register.

CHECK NO.	DATE	CHECKS ISSUED TO OR DESCRIPTION OF DEPOSIT	AMOUNT OF CHECK		✔	AMOUNT OF DEPOSIT		BALANCE 348	56
–	12/22	ATM Withdrawal	40	00				308	56

Steve Pollard made the following transaction at his bank's automated teller machine. Study the transaction record and answer the questions below.

SAVE TIME TELLER
Farmers First Bank

TRANSACTION: Deposit   LOCATION: Gallee

CARD NUMBER: 0276494   ACCOUNT: Savings #002-9189

ATM NUMBER: 0589   AMOUNT: $105.00

DATE: 12/16/97   NEW BALANCE: $465.23

TIME: 5:15 p.m.

---

1. What type of transaction did Steve make, a deposit or a withdrawal? _____

2. At what bank does Steve have this account?

_____

3. What is Steve's account number? _____

4. How much money did Steve deposit or withdraw?

_____

5. What was Steve's balance after this transaction?

_____

Record this transaction in Steve's passbook.

DATE	WITHDRAWAL	DEPOSIT	INTEREST	BALANCE
12/2	25.00			360.23

Cashing and Depositing Checks

Before Carla cashed a check at the bank, she had to *endorse* it. This means she signed her name on the back of the check. She usually waited until she got to the bank to endorse a check. She knew that if someone found her endorsed check, that person could try to cash it.

When Carla endorsed a check, she signed her name just the way it was written on the front. By endorsing it this way, she could *cash* the check— take the money for it. Or she could deposit part or all of it into her account.

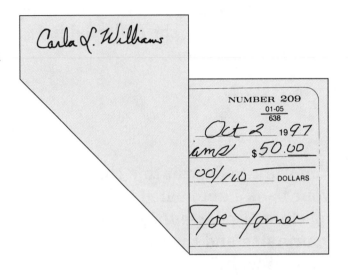

Sometimes Carla needed to endorse a check when she wasn't going to the bank. Then she wrote the words "For Deposit Only" in addition to her name. This way, no one else could cash her check.

These are some of the times you would endorse a check with "For Deposit Only":

- When you deposit a check without asking for any cash back.
- When you mail a deposit to your bank.
- When you deposit a check at an automated teller machine.
- When you give a check to someone else to deposit for you.

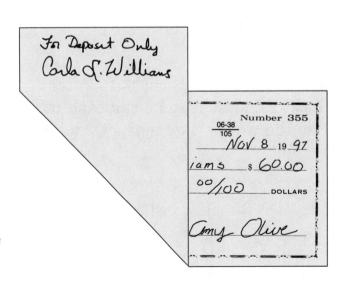

Carla had a check that was made out to her for $10.00. She wanted to give the $10.00 to her friend, Mary Rossi. Since Mary was going to the bank, Carla endorsed the check so Mary could cash it. To do this, she wrote the words "Pay to the Order of" followed by Mary's name. When Mary cashed the check, she endorsed it with her own name.

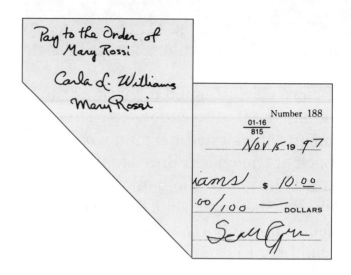

You want to deposit this check at your bank's automated teller machine. Endorse the check with your name and the words "For Deposit Only."

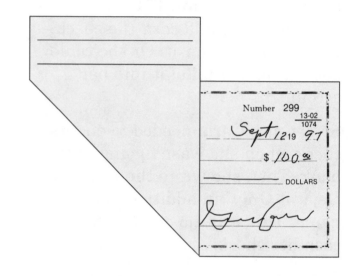

You are giving this check to Peter Rock. Endorse it so he can cash it. Use the words "Pay to the Order of."

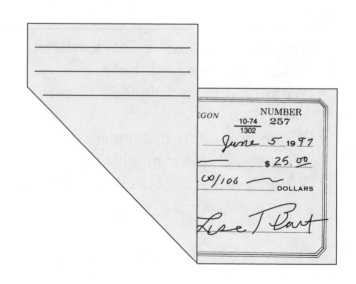

The Bank Statement

Once a month Carla's bank sent her a *bank statement*. The statement listed all the deposits and withdrawals Carla made during the past month. It also listed the check numbers and amounts of all the checks she wrote. The statement showed how much money she had at the beginning and at the end of the month.

Here is the bank statement Carla got for the month of April.

❶ **Closing date.** All the transactions listed on this statement were made before this date.

❷ **Beginning balance.** Carla had $302.75 in this account at the beginning of the month.

❸ **Checks.** This part lists all the checks Carla wrote that have been canceled. The checks are listed in order by check number.

❹ **Other charges.** This part lists all the withdrawals Carla made at the bank's ATM.

❺ **Deposits.** The statement lists the deposits Carla made, both at the ATM and at the bank.

United National Bank
Hometown, Illinois 62000

STATEMENT

Carla Williams
7294 West Street
Hometown, Illinois 62000

❶ Closing Date: 4/30/97
❷ Beginning Balance: 302.75

CHECKING ACCOUNT NUMBER: 618-51-06

❸ **CHECKS**

Check Number	Date Paid	Amount	Check Number	Date Paid	Amount
298	4/3/97	17.84			
299	4/8/97	25.19			
300	4/9/97	10.50			
301	4/14/97	55.58			
*					
303	4/26/97	115.00			

❹ **OTHER CHARGES**

	Date	Amount
WITHDRAWAL ATM 0838	4/12/97	40.00

❺ **DEPOSITS**

Date	Amount	Date	Amount
4/7/97	104.93		
4/21/97	209.86		

❻ Ending Balance: 353.43

❻ **Ending balance.** After all her deposits, withdrawals, and service charges were counted, Carla had $357.11 in her account.

Here is another bank statement. Study it and answer the questions below.

1. How many canceled checks are listed?

   _____

2. What was the amount of the deposit made on 11/10/97?

   _____

3. What is the check number of the check that has not yet been canceled? (Space is marked with a star.)

   _____

4. On what date did Sandy Jackson withdraw $40.00 from the ATM?

   _____

5. How much was Sandy's ending balance on this statement?

   _____

6. How much is the service charge for Sandy's checking account?

   _____

7. What is the total amount of all the canceled checks on this statement?

   _____

UNITED NATIONAL BANK
Hometown, Illinois 62000
STATEMENT

Sandy Jackson
392 Aspen Street
Antioch, Illinois 62001

Closing Date: 11/30/97
Beginning Balance: 453.88

CHECKING ACCOUNT NUMBER: 009-73852

CHECKS

Check Number	Date Paid	Amount	Check Number	Date Paid	Amount
398	11/2/97	63.85			
399	11/5/97	206.37			
400	11/10/97	10.00			
401	11/16/97	26.54			
*					
403	11/20/97	140.00			
404	11/28/97	73.79			

OTHER CHARGES	Date	Amount
WITHDRAWAL ATM 9004	11/25/97	40.00
WITHDRAWAL ATM 0839	11/29/97	20.00
SERVICE CHARGE	11/30/97	5.00

DEPOSITS			
Date	Amount	Date	Amount
11/10/97	204.06		
11/24/97	265.98		

Ending Balance: 338.37

Balancing the Checking Account

The balance in Carla's checkbook register did not usually match the closing balance on her statement. Carla knew why. She always subtracted the amount of each check from her balance. But not every check she wrote was canceled before the statement's closing date.

If a check wasn't canceled, the bank didn't subtract it from Carla's balance. So the balance on the statement was different than the balance in the register.

Carla still used the information on her statement. She used it to make sure both she and the bank recorded everything correctly. This is called *balancing the account*.

Balancing a checking account is not easy. It takes a lot of practice. These two pages will give you an idea of how it can be done.

CHECK NO.	DATE	CHECKS ISSUED TO OR DESCRIPTION OF DEPOSIT	AMOUNT OF CHECK		✔	AMOUNT OF DEPOSIT		BALANCE	
								302	75
298	4/3	Graham Telephone	17	84	✔			284	91
	4/7	deposit				104	93	389	84
299	4/8	Famished Foods	25	19	✔			364	65
300	4/9	King's Way	10	50	✔			354	15
	4/12	ATM Withdrawal	40	00	✔			314	15
301	4/14	Bliss Jewelers	55	58	✔			258	57
302	4/20	General Oil (charge card payment)	32	60				225	97
	4/21	deposit				209	86	435	83
303	4/26	Rachel Isaacson	115	00	✔			320	83
304	5/2	Solestruck Shoe Store	32	64				288	19
	5/5	deposit				89	83	378	02

When Carla balanced her checking account, she first looked at her checkbook register. She put a mark next to each check that appeared on her statement. She made sure the amount of each check in her checkbook register matched the amount on her statement.

Two checks in Carla's register were not on her statement. Checks not listed on the statement are called *outstanding checks*.

On the back of Carla's checkbook register, there were directions to help her balance her account. Here is how Carla followed the directions.

❶ Carla wrote down the check number and amount of each outstanding check. Then she added to get the total. (Remember, outstanding checks appeared in her register, but not on the statement.)

❷ Carla wrote down the ending balance, shown on the front of the statement.

❶ Outstanding Checks	
Number	Amount
302	32.60
304	32.64
Total	65.24

❷ Ending balance on this bank statement	$ 353.43
❸ ADD any deposits in check register not shown on this bank statement	$ 89.83
❹ Total	$ 443.26
❺ SUBTRACT total outstanding checks	$ 65.24
❻ BALANCE	378.02

❸ In Carla's checkbook register, there was one deposit that didn't appear on the statement. She had made this deposit after the closing date of the statement. Carla wrote down the amount of the deposit in the space.

❹ Carla added together the ending balance and the deposit.

❺ She subtracted the total of the outstanding checks.

❻ The amount on this line matched the balance in Carla's checkbook register. Carla's checking account *balanced.*

You won't always be able to balance your account the first time you try. You may need to check for mistakes in addition or subtraction. Sometimes it still won't balance, even after you try many times. Then you may need to ask the bank to help you.

The money in your savings account is used by the bank (or savings and loan institution) to make loans to other people. In return for using your money, the bank pays you interest. The interest you get is a *percent* (%) of the amount in your account.

Percent is a way of figuring in *hundredths*.

1% (one percent) is $\frac{1}{100}$ (one-hundredth).

2% (two percent) is $\frac{2}{100}$ (two-hundredths).

3% (three percent) is $\frac{3}{100}$ (three-hundredths).

Percent can also be written as a decimal fraction. For example, to change 3% to a decimal fraction, drop the percent sign (%) and put the decimal point *two places to the left*.

$$3\% = .03 \text{ (three-hundredths)}$$

To change 12% to a decimal fraction, follow the same steps. Drop the percent sign and put the decimal point *two places to the left*.

$$12\% = .12 \text{ (twelve-hundredths)}$$

Change these percents to decimal fractions. Drop the percent sign and put the decimal point two places to the left.

1. 4% __.04__   2. 11% _____   3. 5% _____   4. 13% __.13__   5. 9% _____

6. 8% _____   7. 22% _____   8. 1% _____   9. 19% _____   10. 43% _____

11. 18% _____   12. 60% _____   13. 37% _____   14. 6% _____   15. 20% _____

Your money earns interest at a yearly or
monthly rate depending on the type of
account you open.

Let's say you have $100.00 in your savings
account. And let's say the bank pays 5%
interest a year. How much interest will you
get? To find out, first change 5% to a
decimal fraction. Then multiply the amount
in your account by the decimal fraction.

There are a total of four numbers after
the decimal points in the problem, so the
decimal point in the answer goes *four
places to the left.*

$5\% = .05$

$$\begin{array}{r} \$100.00 \\ \times\ .05 \\ \hline \$5.0000 \end{array}$$

$\$5.00\cancel0\cancel0$

Cross out the last two zeros. The interest
on $100.00 at 5% is $5.00.

Figure the interest on each amount here. Change the
percent to a decimal fraction. Then multiply the amount by
the decimal fraction. Be sure to put the decimal point in the
right place in your answers.

1. $200.00 at 5% = $10.00
$$\begin{array}{r} \$200.00 \\ \times\ \ .05 \\ \hline 10.00\cancel0\cancel0 \\ \$10.00 \end{array}$$

2. $100.00 at 6% = _____

3. $300.00 at 7% = _____

4. $200.00 at 6% = _____

5. $400.00 at 7% = _____

6. $300.00 at 5% = _____

7. $100.00 at 7% = _____

8. $200.00 at 7% = _____

9. $300.00 at 6% = _____

Interest

Figure the interest on each amount here. Change the percent to a decimal fraction. Then multiply the amount by the decimal fraction. Be sure to put the decimal point in the right place in your answers. You may use a calculator.

1. $250.00 at 5% = $12.50

$$
\begin{array}{r}
\$250.00 \\
\times \quad .05 \\
\hline
12.50\cancel{0}\cancel{0} \\
\$12.50
\end{array}
$$

2. $350.00 at 7% = _____

3. $200.00 at 6% = _____

4. $150.00 at 5% = _____

5. $400.00 at 8% = _____

6. $125.00 at 6% = _____

7. $250.00 at 6% = _____

8. $325.00 at 7% = _____

9. $175.00 at 5% = _____

10. $420.00 at 8% = _____

11. $280.00 at 5% = _____

12. $440.00 at 9% = _____

13. $134.00 at 5% = _____

14. $268.00 at 6% = _____

15. $166.00 at 7% = _____

16. $324.00 at 5% = _____

17. $239.00 at 8% = _____

18. $109.00 at 6% = _____

Figure the interest on the amount in the center of each
wheel at the interest rates between the spokes.

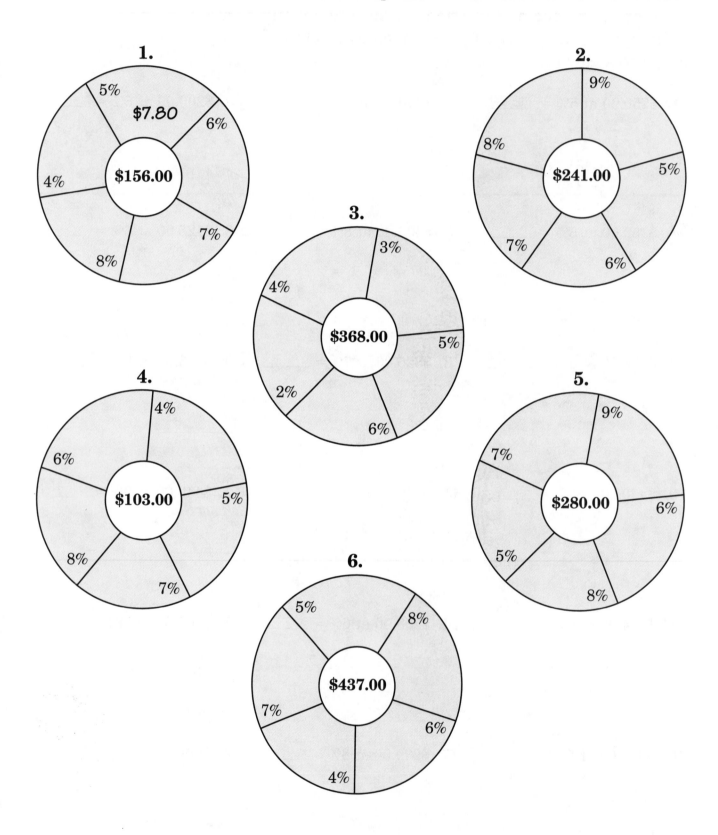

Steve Pollard liked working at The Sandwich House. He liked meeting people. As a waiter, Steve met a lot of people every day.

Part of Steve's job was figuring the total cost of each order. He listed everything that was ordered and added the price of each thing. This amount he wrote in the *subtotal* box of the bill.

Next, Steve figured the sales tax. The sales tax was 6% of the subtotal. He added the sales tax to the subtotal to get the total.

Steve used a table that showed him what 6% of the subtotal was. He also knew how to figure 6% without using a table. Here is how Steve figured the tax on a subtotal of $4.00.

He changed 6% to a decimal fraction.

6% = .06

Then he multiplied the subtotal by the decimal fraction. He moved the decimal point *four places to the left* in his answer and dropped the last two zeros.

$4.00 **subtotal**
× .06
$.2400 **sales tax**

$4.00 **subtotal**
+ .24 **sales tax**
$4.24 **total**

The sales tax on $4.00 is $.24. Steve added $.24 to the subtotal to get the total—$4.24.

The Sandwich House	
ORDER	COST
1 sandwich special	$3.15
1 milk	.85
SUBTOTAL	$4.00
SALES TAX	.24
TOTAL	$4.24

Add the orders on each bill to get the subtotal. Figure 6% sales tax for the subtotal. Add the sales tax to the subtotal to get the total. You may use a calculator.

1.

The Sandwich House

ORDER	COST
1 cheese sandwich	$3.25
1 orange drink	.85
1 pie	1.90
SUBTOTAL	
SALES TAX	
TOTAL	

2.

The Sandwich House

ORDER	COST
1 turkey sandwich	$4.20
1 soup	1.75
1 salad	2.20
1 coffee	.95
SUBTOTAL	
SALES TAX	
TOTAL	

3.

The Sandwich House

ORDER	COST
1 chicken sandwich	$4.15
1 cheese sandwich	3.25
1 fruit plate	3.50
1 milk	.85
1 orange drink	.85
SUBTOTAL	
SALES TAX	
TOTAL	

4.

The Sandwich House

ORDER	COST
2 ham sandwiches	$8.60
1 fruit plate	3.50
1 soup	1.75
3 milks	2.55
1 salad	2.20
2 pie	3.80
SUBTOTAL	
SALES TAX	
TOTAL	

Shopping Quiz

Figure 5% sales tax for each of these things. Add the sales tax to the price to get the total cost. You may use a calculator.

1.
Price $6.60
Sales tax ____.33___
Total ____$6.93____

2.
Price $5.00
Sales tax _____
Total _____

3.
Price $3.20
Sales tax _____
Total _____

4.
Price $24.40
Sales tax _____
Total _____

5.
Price $10.00
Sales tax _____
Total _____

6.
Price $18.00
Sales tax _____
Total _____

7.
Price $28.80
Sales tax _____
Total _____

8.
Price $48.00
Sales tax _____
Total _____

9.
Price $24.40
Sales tax _____
Total _____

10.

Price $20.80

Sales tax _____

Total _____

11.

Price $31.80

Sales tax _____

Total _____

12.

Price $48.00

Sales tax _____

Total _____

13.

Price $22.20

Sales tax _____

Total _____

14.

Price $26.80

Sales tax _____

Total _____

15.

Price $52.60

Sales tax _____

Total _____

16.

Price $86.80

Sales tax _____

Total _____

17.

Price $54.40

Sales tax _____

Total _____

18.

Price $85.80

Sales tax _____

Total _____

SLEEPING BAG

19.

Price $61.00

Sales tax _____

Total _____

20.

Price $98.50

Sales tax _____

Total _____

21.

Price $190.80

Sales tax _____

Total _____

25% Off!

Gant's Department Store was going to have a sale. Everything on sale would be 25% off the regular price.

If the regular price of a hair dryer was $24.95, what would the sale price be?

First change 25% to a decimal fraction.

$25\% = .25$

Then multiply the regular price by the fraction. Move the decimal point four places to the left.

$$
\begin{array}{r}
\$\ 24.95 \\
\times\ .25 \\
\hline
1\ 24\ 75 \\
4\ 99\ 0 \\
\hline
\$6.23\ 75
\end{array}
$$

Now round off your answer. Since the third number to the right of the decimal point (7) is greater than 5, round off to the next highest cent. Drop the last two numbers, and your answer is $6.24.

$\$6.23\cancel{75} = \$6.24$

Subtract $6.24 from the regular price to get the sale price. The sale price of the hair dryer is $18.71.

$$
\begin{array}{r}
\$24.95 \\
-\ 6.24 \\
\hline
\$18.71
\end{array}
$$

To round off numbers to the nearest cent, remember: If the third number to the right of the decimal point is 5 or more, round off your answer to the next highest cent. If the third number to the right of the decimal point is less than 5, just drop the last two numbers.

Figure the sale price of each thing below. First find 25% of the regular price. Round off your answer to the nearest cent. Then subtract that amount from the regular price to get the sale price.

1.

Regular $21.25

25% off ____5.31____

Sale price $15.94

2.

Regular $22.40

25% off _____

Sale price _____

3.

Regular $9.80

25% off _____

Sale price _____

4.

Regular $25.75

25% off _____

Sale price _____

5.

Regular $12.89

25% off _____

Sale price _____

6.

Regular $37.50

25% off _____

Sale price _____

7.

Regular $14.95

25% off _____

Sale price _____

8.

Regular $16.37

25% off _____

Sale price _____

9.

Regular $12.76

25% off _____

Sale price _____

10.

Regular $24.95

25% off _____

Sale price _____

11.

Regular $19.99

25% off _____

Sale price _____

12.

Regular $45.00

25% off _____

Sale price _____

NAME _____

Here are some of the things sold in Gant's Department Store. The store's cost for each thing is shown. The owner of the store wants to make 28% profit on these things. Figure the selling price of each thing by adding the cost and the profit. Write your answers in the blanks.

1.

Cost $10.80

28% Profit _3.02_

Price   _$13.82_

2.

Cost $6.99

28% Profit _____

Price   _____

3.

Cost $12.11

28% Profit _____

Price   _____

4.

Cost $41.55

28% Profit _____

Price   _____

5.

Cost $37.11

28% Profit _____

Price   _____

6.

Cost $45.16

28% Profit _____

Price   _____

7.

Cost $13.25

28% Profit _____

Price   _____

8.

Cost $12.89

28% Profit _____

Price   _____

9.

Cost $79.00

28% Profit _____

Price   _____

Here are some other things the store sells for different profit percents. Figure the price of each one.

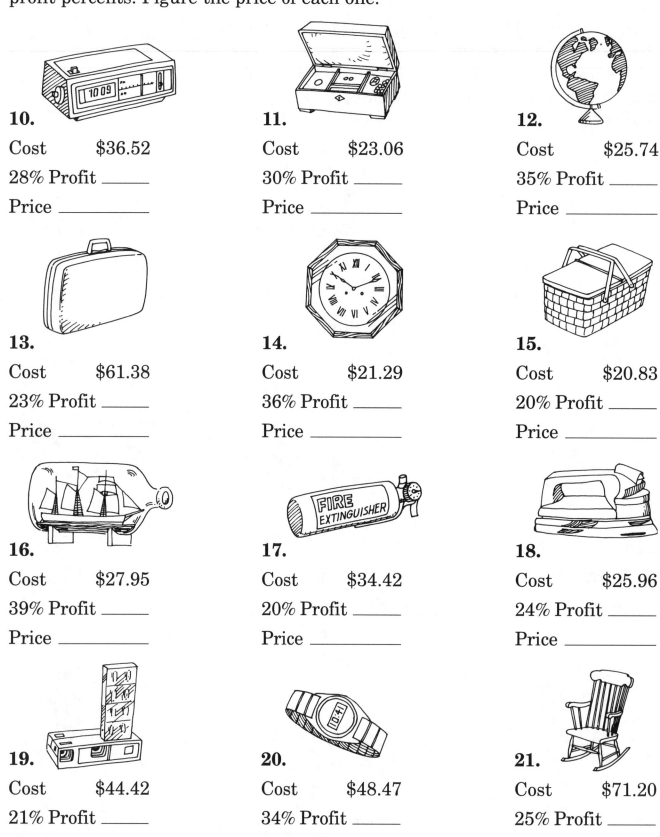

10.

Cost $36.52

28% Profit _____

Price _____

11.

Cost $23.06

30% Profit _____

Price _____

12.

Cost $25.74

35% Profit _____

Price _____

13.

Cost $61.38

23% Profit _____

Price _____

14.

Cost $21.29

36% Profit _____

Price _____

15.

Cost $20.83

20% Profit _____

Price _____

16.

Cost $27.95

39% Profit _____

Price _____

17.

Cost $34.42

20% Profit _____

Price _____

18.

Cost $25.96

24% Profit _____

Price _____

19.

Cost $44.42

21% Profit _____

Price _____

20.

Cost $48.47

34% Profit _____

Price _____

21.

Cost $71.20

25% Profit _____

Price _____

NAME _____

Find the answers to these percent problems. Show your work below each problem and write the answer in the blank. Be sure to put your decimal point in the right place. Round off your answers to the nearest cent. You may use a calculator.

1. 5% of $7.52 = __$.38__

2. 9% of $9.87 = _____

3. 6% of $5.14 = _____

4. 5% of $12.70 = _____

5. 7% of $15.32 = _____

6. 8% of $14.99 = _____

7. 12% of $23.33 = _____

8. 11% of $27.09 = _____

9. 18% of $30.76 = _____

10. 8% of $258.00 = _____

11. 9% of $169.00 = _____

12. 7% of $612.00 = _____

13. 25% of $46.98 = _____

14. 20% of $75.55 = _____

15. 45% of $84.32 = _____

Start with the store's cost of each thing below. Add the store's profit. Subtract the sale amount. Then add the sales tax to get the total cost.

	STORE'S COST	SELLING PRICE	SALE PRICE	TOTAL COST
1.	$20.00	Add 35% profit $27.00	Subtract 10% $24.30	Add 6% sales tax $25.76
2.	$34.00	Add 15% profit	Subtract 12%	Add 5% sales tax
3.	$68.00	Add 18% profit	Subtract 9%	Add 7% sales tax
4.	$119.00	Add 22% profit	Subtract 15%	Add 4% sales tax
5.	$247.00	Add 15% profit	Subtract 5%	Add 6% sales tax

NAME _____

Steve Pollard spent part of his earnings on groceries. Sometimes he needed to divide to find out what something cost.

Steve bought $\frac{1}{2}$ dozen eggs. They were on sale for $.98 per dozen. To find the price of $\frac{1}{2}$ dozen, Steve divided by 2—the bottom number of the fraction $\frac{1}{2}$.

$$
\begin{array}{r}
\$.49 \text{ price per } \frac{1}{2} \text{ dozen} \\
2)\overline{\$.98} \text{ price per dozen} \\
-8 \\
\hline
18 \\
-18 \\
\hline
0
\end{array}
$$

Steve also bought $\frac{1}{4}$ pound of lunch meat. Lunch meat costs $3.96 per pound. To find the cost for $\frac{1}{4}$ pound, Steve divided by 4—the bottom number of the fraction $\frac{1}{4}$.

$$
\begin{array}{r}
\$\ .99 \text{ price per } \frac{1}{4} \text{ pound} \\
4)\overline{\$3.96} \text{ price per pound} \\
-3\,6 \\
\hline
36 \\
-36 \\
\hline
0
\end{array}
$$

Figure the cost of each of these things. (Use the Common Fractions on page 128 to help you see the amount of each fraction.)

1.
$\frac{1}{2}$ pound = $__1.24__

2.
$\frac{1}{4}$ pound = $_____

3.
$\frac{1}{2}$ pound = $_____

4.
$\frac{1}{3}$ pound = $_____

5.
$\frac{1}{2}$ pound = $_____

6.
$\frac{1}{2}$ pound = $_____

7.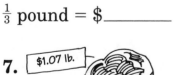
$\frac{1}{4}$ pound = $_____

8.
$\frac{1}{2}$ pound = $_____

9.
$\frac{1}{8}$ pound = $_____

10.

¼ pound = $_____

11.

⅓ pound = $_____

12.

¼ pound = $_____

13.

½ pound = $_____

14.

¼ pound = $_____

15.

⅛ pound = $_____

16.

½ pound = $_____

17.

¼ pound = $_____

18.

⅓ pound = $_____

19.

¼ pound = $_____

20.

⅛ pound = $_____

21.

¼ pound = $_____

22.

⅓ pound = $_____

23.

½ pound = $_____

24.

⅓ pound = $_____

Buying Fabric

Gant's Department Store was having a sale on fabric. It sold fabric by the yard, but many people bought less than a yard.

One kind of fabric cost $3.76 per yard. Mary Rossi, a friend of Carla's, bought $\frac{3}{4}$ yard to make a shirt. How much did it cost? To find out, first divide the cost per yard by 4. Your answer is the cost of $\frac{1}{4}$ yard.

Next multiply the cost of $\frac{1}{4}$ yard by 3—the top number in the fraction $\frac{3}{4}$. Your answer is the cost of $\frac{3}{4}$ yard.

```
     $ .94   cost of ¼ yard
 4)$3.76     cost per yard
  - 3 6
     16
   - 16
      0
```

```
  $ .94   cost of ¼ yard
   × 3
  $2.82   cost of ¾ yard
```

Find the cost of $\frac{3}{4}$ yard of each of these fabrics.

1. $5.88 yd.

$\frac{3}{4}$ yard = $ _4.41_

2. $3.92

$\frac{3}{4}$ yard = $ _____

3. $8.96

$\frac{3}{4}$ yard = $ _____

4. $4.12

$\frac{3}{4}$ yard = $ _____

5. $9.88

$\frac{3}{4}$ yard = $ _____

6. $5.32

$\frac{3}{4}$ yard = $ _____

7. $4.80

$\frac{3}{4}$ yard = $ _____

8. $12.48

$\frac{3}{4}$ yard = $ _____

9. $3.52

$\frac{3}{4}$ yard = $ _____

Another kind of fabric cost $5.61 per yard. Mary bought $\frac{2}{3}$ yard. How much did it cost? To find out, first divide the cost per yard by 3. Your answer is the cost of $\frac{1}{3}$ yard.

$$
\begin{array}{r}
\$1.87 \quad \text{price for } \frac{1}{3} \text{ yard} \\
3\overline{)\$5.61} \quad \text{price per yard} \\
\underline{-3} \\
2\,6 \\
\underline{-2\,4} \\
21 \\
\underline{-21} \\
0
\end{array}
$$

Next, multiply the cost of $\frac{1}{3}$ yard by 2. Your answer is the cost of $\frac{2}{3}$ yard.

$$
\begin{array}{r}
\$1.87 \quad \text{cost per } \frac{1}{3} \text{ yard} \\
\times\, 2 \\
\hline
\$3.74 \quad \text{cost of } \frac{2}{3} \text{ yard}
\end{array}
$$

Find the cost of $\frac{2}{3}$ yard of each of these fabrics.

10. $4.41 yd.

$\frac{2}{3}$ yard = $ 2.94

11. $7.89

$\frac{2}{3}$ yard = $_____

12. $9.00

$\frac{2}{3}$ yard = $_____

13. $11.97

$\frac{2}{3}$ yard = $_____

14. $6.33

$\frac{2}{3}$ yard = $_____

15. $15.99

$\frac{2}{3}$ yard = $_____

16. $5.70

$\frac{2}{3}$ yard = $_____

17. $10.59

$\frac{2}{3}$ yard = $_____

18. $6.69

$\frac{2}{3}$ yard = $_____

NAME _____

Figure the cost of each of these things. Write your answers in the blanks.

1.

$\frac{3}{8}$ lb. = $ _____.33_____
(pound)

2.

$\frac{3}{5}$ lb. = $ _____

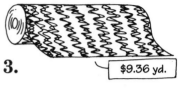

3.

$\frac{3}{4}$ yard = $ _____

4.

$\frac{5}{8}$ lb. = $ _____

5.

$\frac{3}{8}$ lb. = $ _____

6.

$\frac{4}{5}$ lb. = $ _____

7.

$\frac{5}{6}$ yard = $ _____

8.

$\frac{7}{8}$ lb. = $ _____

9.

$\frac{4}{5}$ lb. = $ _____

10.

$\frac{3}{8}$ lb. = $ _____

11.

$\frac{7}{8}$ yard = $ _____

12.

$\frac{3}{4}$ lb. = $ _____

13.

$\frac{2}{3}$ lb. = $ _____

14.

$\frac{5}{6}$ lb. = $ _____

15.

$\frac{5}{8}$ lb. = $ _____

Figure the cost of each of these things. Write your
answers in the blanks. Look at the example below.

$2\frac{3}{4}$ lb. = $ ___2.42___

88¢ lb.

$$\begin{array}{r} \$.22 \\ 4\overline{)\$.88} \\ -8 \\ \hline 08 \\ -8 \\ \hline 0 \end{array}$$

$$\begin{array}{r} \$.22 \\ \times 3 \\ \hline \$.66 = \frac{3}{4} \text{ lb.} \end{array} \rightarrow$$

$$\begin{array}{r} \$ .88 \\ \times 2 \text{ lbs.} \\ \hline \$1.76 \text{ for 2 lbs.} \end{array} \rightarrow$$

$$\begin{array}{r} \$1.76 \\ + .66 \\ \hline \$2.42 \text{ for } 2\frac{3}{4} \text{ lbs.} \end{array}$$

$4.24 lb.

1.

$2\frac{3}{8}$ lb. = $ _____

$3.84
Per lb.

2.

$1\frac{7}{8}$ lb. = $ _____

$4.28 lb.

3.

$3\frac{3}{4}$ lb. = $ _____

$1.28 lb.

4.

$2\frac{1}{4}$ lb. = $ _____

15¢ lb.

5.

$6\frac{3}{5}$ lb. = $ _____

35¢ lb.

6.

$4\frac{4}{5}$ lb. = $ _____

$3.84 lb.

7.

$3\frac{1}{8}$ lb. = $ _____

88¢ lb.

8.

$2\frac{3}{4}$ lb. = $ _____

18¢ lb.

9.

$9\frac{2}{3}$ lb. = $ _____

64¢ lb.

10.

$5\frac{3}{8}$ lb. = $ _____

$1.44
Per lb.

11.

$2\frac{5}{8}$ lb. = $ _____

96¢ lb.

12.

$3\frac{3}{4}$ lb. = $ _____

NAME _____

Steve Pollard needed to buy tomatoes for The Sandwich House. Steve always bought his tomatoes at Farmer's Yard. He usually bought so many that Farmer's Yard gave him a special price of 64¢ a pound. Figure the cost of each basket below. Write your answers in the blanks.

1.

$3\frac{1}{2}$ pounds = $ ___2.24___

2.

$5\frac{3}{4}$ pounds = $_____

3.

$9\frac{1}{4}$ pounds = $_____

4.

$12\frac{3}{8}$ pounds = $_____

5.

$14\frac{1}{2}$ pounds = $_____

6.

$15\frac{5}{8}$ pounds = $_____

7.

$17\frac{1}{4}$ pounds = $_____

8.

$20\frac{3}{4}$ pounds = $_____

9.

$21\frac{3}{8}$ pounds = $_____

10.

$24\frac{1}{2}$ pounds = $_____

Money Problems

Count the money on the left side of the page. Write the total amount in the first blank on the right side of the page. Then find the fraction of that amount asked for. Write that amount in the second blank.

1.

Total amount = $_____

$\frac{3}{4}$ of amount = $_____

2.

Total amount = $_____

$\frac{2}{3}$ of amount = $_____

3.

Total amount = $_____

$\frac{7}{8}$ of amount = $_____

4.

Total amount = $_____

$\frac{2}{5}$ of amount = $_____

In June, Carla Williams finished school and started working full time for Runaway Sports Shop. Her boss, Mr. Swift, was very pleased with Carla's work and made her an assistant manager. He also gave her a raise. Carla now earned $8.20 an hour. She worked 40 hours a week. Sometimes Mr. Swift asked Carla to work more than 40 hours a week. This is called working *overtime*.

For every hour over 40 that Carla worked in a week, Mr. Swift paid her *time-and-a-half.* Time-and-a-half means that for every hour Carla worked overtime, she earned her regular hourly wage plus half that amount.

Here is how Carla figured how much she earned an hour at time-and-a-half.

$$\begin{array}{r} \$4.10 \\ \hline 2)\overline{\$8.20} \end{array}$$ **half of hourly wage**
hourly wage

$$\begin{array}{r} \$8.20 \\ + \$4.10 \\ \hline \$12.30 \end{array}$$ **hourly wage**
half of hourly wage
time-and-a-half

One week Carla worked 46 hours. For the first 40 hours, she earned her regular hourly wage. For the last 6 hours, she earned time-and-a-half. Here is how Carla figured how much she earned for the week.

$$\begin{array}{r} \$8.20 \\ \times \quad 40 \\ \hline \$328.00 \end{array}$$ **hourly wage**
hours worked
regular wages

$$\begin{array}{r} \$12.30 \\ \times \quad 6 \\ \hline \$73.80 \end{array}$$ **time-and-a-half wage**
overtime hours worked
time-and-a-half wages

$$\begin{array}{r} \$328.00 \\ + 73.80 \\ \hline \$401.80 \end{array}$$ **regular wages**
time-and-a-half wages
total wages

Another week, Carla worked 43 hours. Answer these questions about how much she earned that week. Remember, Carla's regular hourly wage is now $8.20.

1. How many hours did Carla work at her regular hourly wage? _____

2. How much did Carla earn at her regular wage? _____

3. How many hours overtime did Carla work? _____

4. How much did Carla earn at the time-and-a-half wage? _____

5. How much did Carla earn altogether for 43 hours' work? _____

One week, Runaway Sports Shop had a big sale. The store was very busy, so Carla worked overtime. That week, Carla worked 48 hours. Answer these questions about how much she earned that week.

6. How many hours did Carla work at her regular hourly wage? _____

7. How much did Carla earn at her regular wage? _____

8. How many hours overtime did Carla work? _____

9. How much did Carla earn at the time-and-a-half wage? _____

10. How much did Carla earn altogether for 48 hours' work? _____

The hours Carla worked in six weeks are shown below. Her regular wage is $8.20 an hour. She gets time-and-a-half for working overtime (more than 40 hours a week). Fill in the blanks to show how much Carla earned each week.

Week Ending	Hours Worked	Regular Earnings	Time-and-a-Half Earnings	Total Earnings
8/3	40			
8/10	42			
8/17	45			
8/24	38			
8/31	41			
9/7	44			

Answer these questions about Carla's earnings.

1. Did Carla get paid overtime every week? _____

2. For which weeks did Carla earn time-and-a-half? _____

3. For which week did Carla earn the most money? _____

4. For which week did Carla earn the least money? _____

5. For which week did Carla earn the most overtime? _____

6. How many hours did Carla work overtime during the six weeks? _____

7. How much did she earn in time-and-a-half wages during the six weeks? _____

8. Carla deposited $\frac{3}{4}$ of her time-and-a-half earnings in her savings account. How much money did she deposit during the six weeks? _____

The number of hours each of the employees of the Chocolate Factory worked one week is shown below. Anyone who worked overtime (more than 40 hours) gets time-and-a-half for the overtime hours. Figure the time-and-a-half wage for each employee. Then fill in the blanks to show how much each employee earned for the week.

	Employee	Regular Hourly Wage	Time-and-a-Half Hourly Wage	Hours Worked	Regular Earnings	Time-and-a-Half Earnings	Total Earnings
1.	Tom Jay	$5.50		47			
2.	Kay Fox	$5.25		41			
3.	Ed Eng	$6.40		$38\frac{1}{2}$			
4.	Sue Orr	$5.30		43			
5.	Jim Day	$6.60		40			
6.	Roy Wax	$10.00		46			
7.	Joe Zim	$5.40		42			
8.	Ida Lee	$8.00		44			
9.	Al Sax	$5.60		45			
10.	Fay Tut	$6.00		40			
11.	Ben Gee	$7.20		48			
12.	Sal Ott	$5.50		49			
13.	Ike Foy	$6.20		$39\frac{1}{2}$			
14.	Ann Bly	$5.30		47			
15.	Pat Uno	$9.00		50			

Benefits

When Carla started working full time, she began to get *benefits*. This means Runaway Sports Shop paid for part of her health insurance costs. They would also pay for Carla's sick leave and vacation time.

With health insurance, Carla had to pay only a part of her doctor and dentist bills. The insurance plan had a *deductible* of $100. This means Carla would have to pay the first $100 of her bills each calendar year. After that, the insurance company would pay 80% of each bill.

To pay for her part of the insurance, another deduction was taken from Carla's paycheck. Her paycheck now showed these deductions:

REGULAR WAGES	OVERTIME WAGES	TOTAL GROSS WAGES	FEDERAL INCOME TAX	STATE INCOME TAX
$713.40	$86.10	$799.50	$82.00	$31.98

	FICA	MEDICARE	HEALTH INSURANCE	NET WAGES
	$49.57	$11.59	$28.00	$596.36

Carla gets paid twice a month. This means she gets 24 paychecks a year. How much does her health insurance cost her for one month? _____ For one year? _____

Here are the amounts of Carla's doctor and dentist bills for one year. For each bill, figure out how much Carla will pay and how much the insurance company will pay. Write your answers in the blanks.

Bills	Carla pays	Insurance pays
$100 (dentist)	$100 (deductible)	0
	Carla pays 20%	Insurance pays 80%
$70 (dentist)	$14.00	_____
$45 (doctor)	_____	_____
$15 (medicine)	_____	_____

When Carla worked part time, she did not get paid if she was sick and missed work. Now that she worked full time, she could miss some days and still get paid.

Runaway Sports Shop gave full-time employees one-half day of sick leave per month. Carla would earn six days of sick leave each year. She could not build up sick leave from year to year. If she was sick more than six days in any year, she would only get paid for six of those days.

Figure the amount of sick leave Carla will earn. Write your answers in the blanks.

Time worked	Sick leave earned
1 month	$\frac{1}{2}$ day
2 months	_____
3 months	_____
6 months	_____
10 months	_____

Carla also began to earn vacation time. She would earn two weeks vacation each year. After she had worked full time for five years, she would earn three weeks a year.

Carla would have to work full time for six months before she could use any of her vacation. Again, she could not build up vacation time from year to year. If she did not use all of her vacation days within a year, she would lose the days she didn't use.

Figure the amount of vacation Carla can take. Write your answers in the blanks.

Time worked	Vacation earned
5 months	0 weeks
9 months	_____
1 year	_____
5 years	_____

Carla was happy to work overtime at Runaway Sports Shop. She liked her job and earning the overtime money. She was saving her money for a vacation. She planned to visit her sister in New Orleans in February. Her goal was to save $500.00 to pay for the trip. She had six months to save up the money.

To help make saving money fun, Carla drew a thermometer to show how much money she saved. Each time she deposited money in her savings account, she would color in part of the thermometer. When the whole thermometer was colored in, she would have reached her goal. Carla would have saved 100% of the money she needed for her trip. 100% is the whole amount—$500.00.

Carla looked in her savings passbook to see how much money she had already saved. When she first started her savings account she had 10% of her goal. How much money did she have in her savings account?

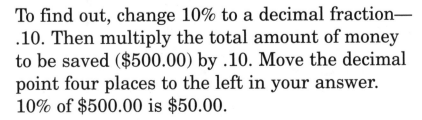

To find out, change 10% to a decimal fraction—.10. Then multiply the total amount of money to be saved ($500.00) by .10. Move the decimal point four places to the left in your answer. 10% of $500.00 is $50.00.

$$10\% = .10$$

$$
\begin{array}{r}
\$500.00 \quad \textbf{total amount} \\
\times\ .10 \\
\hline
\$50.00\cancel{0}\cancel{0} \quad \textbf{10\% of total}
\end{array}
$$

Figure the following percent amounts that Carla saved.
Write each amount next to the thermometer.

1. 15% of $500.00

2. 35% of $500.00

3. 40% of $500.00

4. 55% of $500.00

5. 70% of $500.00

6. 85% of $500.00

Figuring Percent

When Carla began working full time, she was paid twice a month. Figure the following percent amounts that Carla saved from every paycheck for six months. Round off your answers to the nearest cent. Then answer the last two questions.

1. 12% of $596.00 = __$71.52__

$596.00
$$\times \quad .12$$
1192 00
5960 0
$71.52 00

2. 5% of $550.00 = _____

3. 8% of $624.08 = _____

4. 6% of $600.00 = _____

5. 7% of $585.20 = _____

6. 11% of $612.20 = _____

7. 9% of $620.25 = _____

8. 10% of $545.20 = _____

9. 3% of $635.43 = _____

10. 6% of $633.60 = _____

11. 13% of $598.22 = _____

12. 4% of $583.00 = _____

13. How much money did Carla save in six months? _____

14. Did Carla reach her goal of saving $500.00 in six months? _____

In June, Steve Pollard started working full time for The Sandwich House. He worked hard and got to work on time. He was promoted to supervisor. This meant that he was in charge of all the other waiters and waitresses during the time that he worked. When there were problems, he helped solve them. This helped The Sandwich House run smoothly. Because The Sandwich House was doing so well, the owner gave all the employees a raise in monthly pay. Figure the amount of each raise and each employee's new earnings.

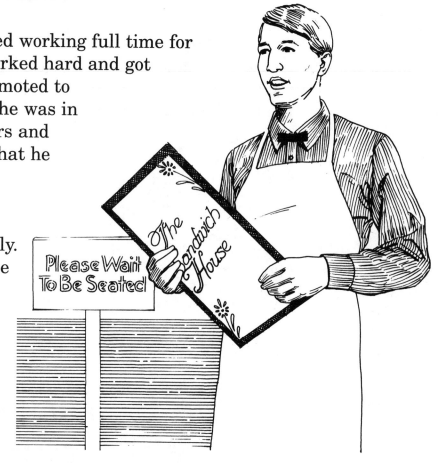

	Employee	Regular Monthly Earnings	Percent Raise	Amount of Raise	Total New Earnings
1.	Steve Pollard	$850.00	21%		
2.	Susan Jones	$880.00	15%		
3.	David Wolfe	$800.00	16%		
4.	Ruth Royer	$850.00	12%		
5.	Kim Lee	$1,100.00	14%		
6.	Mike Bowen	$790.00	20%		
7.	Jose Vega	$875.00	15%		
8.	Mary Wang	$1,000.00	10%		
9.	Nina Perez	$945.00	13%		
10.	John Conner	$870.00	11%		

NAME _____

Like Carla, Steve had been saving part of his earnings. He had saved enough money for a down payment on a used car. But after he bought the car, he had to make car payments every month. So he needed to be very careful about spending his money.

To help keep track of his spending, Steve drew a pie chart. The chart showed about what percent of his take-home pay he spent on different things for one month. Steve's total take-home pay for that month was $1,300.00 (wages, overtime pay, and tips).

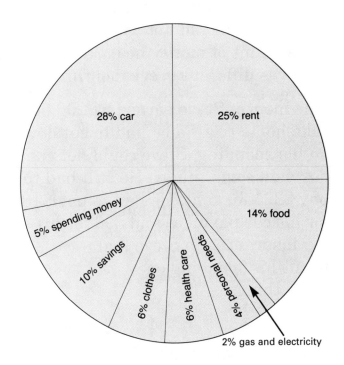

Use the pie chart to answer the questions below. Use $1,300.00 as 100% of Steve's monthly earnings.

1. Steve rented an apartment with a friend. How much money did he spend on rent?

   .25 × $1300 = $325

2. How much money did Steve spend on food? _____

3. How much money did he spend on gas and electricity? _____

4. How much money did Steve spend on personal needs, such as laundry and things from the drugstore? _____

5. How much did he spend on health care for doctor and dentist bills and medicine? _____

6. How much money did Steve spend on clothes? _____

7. How much money did he spend on his car for car payments, gas, and car insurance? _____

8. How much money did Steve deposit in his savings account? _____

9. How much money did Steve have left over for spending money? _____

Steve did not always earn $1,300.00 a month. Sometimes he did not work overtime. And the amount of money he earned in tips was different every month.

One month, Steve earned $1,200.00 in take-home pay. So he had to cut down on his spending. Steve could not cut down on some things. He still had to pay $325 for rent. He had to pay $180 for his car payment and $96 for his car insurance. So Steve had to cut his spending on other things.

?% savings
3% present
1% health care
10% car bill
4% gas
6% clothes
4% personal needs
2% gas & electric
12% food
8% car insurance
27.1% rent
15% car payment

Use the pie chart to answer the questions below. Use the $1,200 as 100% of Steve's monthly earnings.

rent	$325.
car payment	$180.
car insurance	$96.

1. Steve cut down on his food bill by not eating out. How much money did he spend on food? _____
2. He used less electricity that month. How much money did Steve spend on gas and electricity? _____
3. Steve spent a little less on personal needs. How much money did he spend on personal needs? _____
4. Steve bought only the clothes he really needed. How much money did he spend on clothes? _____
5. He saved money on gas by driving less. How much money did Steve spend on gas? _____
6. Steve had to buy some medicine. How much money did he spend on health care? _____
7. Steve's car broke down and he had to pay to fix it. How much money did he spend for his car bill? _____
8. Steve had to buy a present for a good friend. How much money did he spend on the present? _____
9. About how much money did Steve have left for his savings account? _____

Earning Commission

Carla Williams went to Travelon Tours to book her trip to New Orleans. Her friend, Tom Otani, worked there. Tom told Carla how Travelon Tours earned its money.

For every airline ticket Travelon Tours sold, the airline paid them 5% of the cost of the ticket.

For every hotel booking they made, the hotel paid them 10% of the cost of the room.

For every cruise they sold, the cruise company paid them 15% of the cost of the cruise.

The money Travelon Tours earned is called *commission*. Commission is money earned from selling.

The map shows the cost of airline tickets between different cities. The ticket prices are for *one way*. Use the map to figure Travelon Tour's commission on the following bookings.

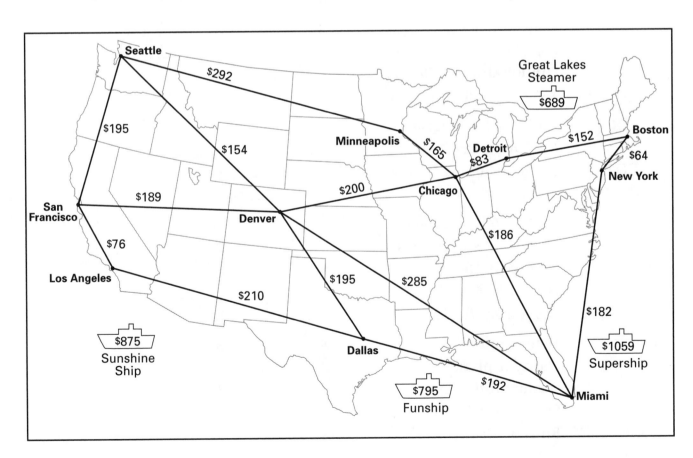

Trip		Bookings	Cost	Commission	Total Commission
1.	AIR	San Francisco to Los Angeles	$ _76.00_	$ _3.80_	
		Los Angeles to San Francisco	$ _76.00_	$ _3.80_	$ _7.60_
2.	AIR	Minneapolis to Seattle	$ _____	$ _____	
		Seattle to Minneapolis	$ _____	$ _____	
	HOTEL	$76 a night for 4 nights	$ _____	$ _____	$ _____
3.	AIR	Chicago to Miami	$ _____	$ _____	
		Miami to Denver	$ _____	$ _____	
		Denver to Chicago	$ _____	$ _____	$ _____
4.	AIR	Boston to Detroit	$ _____	$ _____	
		Detroit to Chicago	$ _____	$ _____	
	CRUISE	Great Lakes Steamer	$ _____	$ _____	$ _____
5.	AIR	Los Angeles to Dallas	$ _____	$ _____	
		Dallas to Miami	$ _____	$ _____	
	HOTEL	$69 a night for 7 nights	$ _____	$ _____	$ _____
6.	AIR	Boston to New York	$ _____	$ _____	
		New York to Miami	$ _____	$ _____	
	CRUISE	Supership Cruise	$ _____	$ _____	$ _____
7.	AIR	Denver to Seattle	$ _____	$ _____	
		Seattle to San Francisco	$ _____	$ _____	
		San Francisco to Denver	$ _____	$ _____	
	HOTEL	$55 a night for 5 nights	$ _____	$ _____	$ _____
8.	AIR	Dallas to Los Angeles	$ _____	$ _____	
		Los Angeles to Dallas	$ _____	$ _____	
	HOTEL	$65 a night for 2 nights	$ _____	$ _____	
	CRUISE	Sunshine Cruise	$ _____	$ _____	$ _____
9.	AIR	Seattle to Minneapolis	$ _____	$ _____	
		Minneapolis to Chicago	$ _____	$ _____	
		Chicago to Denver	$ _____	$ _____	
		Denver to Seattle	$ _____	$ _____	
	HOTEL	$59 a night for 12 nights	$ _____	$ _____	$ _____
10.	AIR	Denver to Dallas	$ _____	$ _____	
		Dallas to Miami	$ _____	$ _____	
		Miami to Denver	$ _____	$ _____	
	HOTEL	$47 a night for 10 nights	$ _____	$ _____	
	CRUISE	Funship Cruise	$ _____	$ _____	$ _____

NAME _____

Late in February, Carla went to Travelon Tours to pay for her trip to New Orleans. Tom Otani gave her the airline ticket. Her ticket showed the time of her flights.

On her flight to New Orleans, Carla had to change planes in St. Louis.

On her flight to Chicago, Carla had to change planes in Memphis.

Travelon Tours
FLIGHT TIMES

February 23

Leave Chicago	7:30 A.M.
Arrive St. Louis	8:30 A.M.
—CHANGE PLANES—	
Leave St. Louis	9:10 A.M.
Arrive New Orleans	11:10 A.M.

March 1

Leave New Orleans	6:50 P.M.
Arrive Memphis	7:50 P.M.
—CHANGE PLANES—	
Leave Memphis	8:40 P.M.
Arrive Chicago	10:10 P.M.

Study the list of Carla's flight times. Then answer the questions below.

1. How long is the flight from Chicago to St. Louis? _____

2. How long is the flight from St. Louis to New Orleans? _____

3. What is the total flying time from Chicago to New Orleans? _____

4. How much time does Carla have in St. Louis to change planes? _____

5. On the return trip, how much time does Carla have in Memphis to change planes? _____

6. What is the total flying time from New Orleans to Chicago? _____

7. What is the total flying time for the round trip? _____

Carla paid for her trip with a check. The cost of the airline ticket for the round trip was $328.00. She had to pay 2% sales tax.

Figure the total cost of Carla's ticket. Then fill out the check below to Travelon Tours for the total amount. Use today's date and sign your name. Then answer the questions below.

```
┌─────────────────────────────────────────────────────────────────┐
│                                                    NUMBER  348    │
│   UNITED NATIONAL BANK                      09-38                  │
│   Hometown, Illinois                        241                    │
│                                             _____ 19 ___ │
│   PAY TO                                                           │
│   THE ORDER OF _____  $ _____    │
│                                                                   │
│   _____ DOLLARS   │
│                         nonnegotiable                             │
│                                                                   │
│                                             _____     │
│   ⑆0241⑆ 0938⑆ 618⑈51⑈06                                          │
└─────────────────────────────────────────────────────────────────┘
```

8. Carla had saved $500.00 for her trip. She planned to spend $\frac{3}{4}$ of her savings on her ticket. How much less than that did she spend? _____

9. What is the one-way cost of the trip? _____

10. Carla's flight from New Orleans to Chicago covered 840 miles. What was the cost per mile? _____

11. In all, the trip was 1,702 air miles. It took 5.5 hours of flying time. How many miles were covered each hour? (Round off your answer to the nearest mile.) _____

12. In New Orleans, Carla took a taxi to her sister's house. The ride was 13.4 miles and cost $18.50. What was the cost per mile? _____

The Weekend Trip

Carla and her sister, Maria, made a weekend trip. They rented a car and drove along the Mississippi River. They spent one night in a hotel. They each paid half the total cost of the trip.

Answer the questions to find out how much the trip cost.

1. Dixie Rent-a-Car charged $38.95 a day for a car. Mileage was free. How much would it cost to rent a car for two days? _____

2. Travelcar charged $24.75 a day and $.25 a mile. The trip was 200 miles. How much would it cost to rent the car for two days? _____

3. The sisters rented a car from the company with the lower price. Which company was that? _____

4. Carla and Maria drove 115 miles and used 4.6 gallons of gas. How many miles per gallon did the car get? _____

5. Carla and Maria stopped for lunch. Add up their bill on the right. They also left a tip that was 15% of the total. How much was the tip?

   _____

RIVERBOAT CAFE	
2 fish specials ($5.95 each)	
2 soft drinks ($.85 each)	
2 pieces of pie ($1.95 each)	
2 coffees ($.85 each)	
Subtotal	
Add 5% tax	
THANK YOU! TOTAL	

6. The hotel cost $56.00 a night. They had to pay 5% tax on the room. How much did the hotel cost altogether? _____

7. That night, the sisters spent $28.75 for dinner. The next day, they spent $12.25 for lunch. For the whole trip, they spent $16.00 for gas. How much did these things cost altogether? _____

8. How much did the sisters spend for the whole trip? _____

9. How much did Carla pay for $\frac{1}{2}$ the total cost of the trip? _____

10. Carla started out with $500.00. She spent $334.56 for her airline ticket and $18.50 for the taxi ride. How much money did she have left after her weekend trip? _____

Take your own trip! Start at the top left square of the maze. Follow the openings through the squares, subtracting the money you spend as you go. Use a calculator. Then fill in the blank at the end of the maze.

	Air ticket to Los Angeles $76.00	Taxi $9.75	Hotel $41.50 a night for 2 nights + 7% tax	Telephone call $3.58
Begin trip with $800.00				
Ski lift ticket $30.00	Tip $2.00	Dinner $13.95 + 7% tax	Tip for waiter $2.25	City tour $20.00
FREE room with friends	Lunch $6.95 + 7% tax	Camp overnight $11.00	Drive with friends to Denver $25.00 for gas	FREE Swimming
Concert ticket $13.50	Taxi $6.75	Hotel $36.00 a night for 1 night + 5% tax	Fast-food lunch $3.25 + 5% tax	3/4 pound of apples $.84/lb.
Air ticket to Seattle $154.00	FREE dinner on plane	Boat trip $18.00	2 rolls of film $2.89 each + 5% tax	Movie $5.50
Money left: $_____	FREE ride home	Special air pass to San Francisco 15% less than $195.00	Tip for waiter $2.00	Dinner $8.85 + 5% tax

NAME _____

Answer these questions.

1. Suppose you work from 3:30 P.M. to 9:00 P.M. each day, Monday through Friday. You take an unpaid break from 6:00 to 6:30. How many hours do you work each week? _____

2. You work in a restaurant. Your hourly wage is $5.25. One evening you work from 5:30 to 9:30 and make $34.20 altogether. How much do you make in tips that evening? _____

3. You just got your first paycheck. The gross amount was $187.15, and the net amount was $150.55. The state tax, FICA, and Medicare totaled $17.60. How much was the federal income tax? _____

4. You buy several tools at a hardware store. The subtotal is $42.50, and the tax is 6%. What is the total cost? _____

5. Your take-home pay is $846.00 per month. You spend $\frac{1}{6}$ of it on your car payment. How much is your car payment? _____

6. You want to buy a co-worker a present. You are collecting money from 14 people at work. You need to collect $37.50. If all 15 of you give the same amount, how much will each person need to give? _____

7. You buy $2\frac{5}{8}$ pounds of salmon at $5.60 a pound. How much do you spend on salmon? _____

8. Suppose your company gives its employees eight days of sick leave each year. You have worked at the company for $1\frac{1}{2}$ years. How many days of sick leave have you earned? _____

9. You are depositing a ten-dollar bill, a one-dollar bill, three quarters, and a check made out to you for $16.92. The bank number on the check is 12-36. Fill out the deposit slip, using today's date.

DEPOSIT SLIP		CASH ➡			
		LIST CHECKS SINGLY			
					01-123 / 1200
		TOTAL			
DATE_____ 19___		LESS CASH RECEIVED			USE OTHER SIDE FOR ADDITIONAL LISTING. ◆ ENTER TOTAL HERE
		TOTAL FROM OTHER SIDE			
SIGN HERE FOR CASH RECEIVED		NET DEPOSIT			BE SURE EACH ITEM IS PROPERLY ENDORSED

CHECKS AND OTHER ITEMS ARE RECEIVED FOR DEPOSIT SUBJECT TO THE PROVISIONS OF THE UNIFORM COMMERCIAL CODE OR ANY APPLICABLE COLLECTION AGREEMENT.

DEPOSITED IN

UNITED NATIONAL BANK
Hometown, Illinois

⑆0241⑈ 0938⑆ 618⑉51⑈06

10. Write each of these entries in the correct column of the passbook below. Figure the new balance after each entry.

Date	Entry	Amount
9/7	Deposit	125.00
9/14	Deposit	50.00
9/15	Interest	(5% of 175.00) ÷ 12
9/28	Withdrawal	30.00
10/12	Deposit	85.00
10/19	Withdrawal	27.00

DATE	WITHDRAWAL	DEPOSIT	INTEREST	BALANCE

Posttest II

Use the arithmetic skills you have learned to do these
problems. Remember to put the decimal point in the
right place in your answers.

1.
```
   25
   86
   47
 + 31
  189
```

2.
```
   40
   98
  102
 + 158
```

3.
```
  986
 − 109
```

4.
```
 $12.46
 ×    3
```

5.
```
 $8.67
 − 4.35
```

6.
```
 $48.89
 ×     9
```

7.
```
 $1.35
  1.48
  9.10
 + 6.55
```

8.
```
 $10.58
   9.64
 + 8.12
```

9. 2)$5.72

10.
```
 $86.32
 − 78.30
```

11. 8)$9.84

12.
```
 $60.40
 − 53.25
```

13.
```
   47
   53
  188
 + 243
```

14.
```
 $4.75
 ×  48
```

15.
```
 $1.50
  2.35
  4.10
 + 6.54
```

16.
```
 $85.46
 − 64.58
```

17. 9)$23.85

18.
```
 $258.63
 + 159.87
```

19.
```
 $45.82
  75.04
  58.67
 + 63.88
```

20.
```
 $126.38
 − 83.92
```

21.
```
 $238.11
 −   8.99
```

22.
```
 $7.99
 ×  67
```

23. 6)$218.64

24.
```
 $5.62
 ×  52
```

25. 7.5)96

26. $356.80
     25.71
   + 9.34

27. 13)$99.19

28. $100.00
    × .01

29. $458.31
  − 258.22

30. $376.80
    × .05

31. 15)$131.10

32. $332.06
  − 306.07

33. $479.00
    × .29

34. $493.09
    122.47
  + 258.58

35. 2.5)21.5

36. $208.86
  − 180.62

37. $123.50
    × .18

38. 7.7)34.65

39. $248.50
    × .64

40. 11.8)749.3

41. Find 75% of $14.52. _____$10.89_____

42. Find 42% of $38.50. _____

43. Find 8% of $17.25. _____

44. Find 10% of $219.00. _____

45. Find 12% of $52.75. _____

46. Find $\frac{1}{2}$ of 980 lb. _____

47. Find $\frac{3}{4}$ of $663.24. _____

48. Find $\frac{5}{8}$ of 152 lb. _____

49. Find $\frac{2}{3}$ of $115.83. _____

50. Find $\frac{3}{8}$ of $29.44. _____

Multiplication Table

Use this multiplication table to help you find the answers
to multiplication problems.

×	1	2	3	4	5	6	7	8	9	10	11	12
1	1	2	3	4	5	6	7	8	9	10	11	12
2	2	4	6	8	10	12	14	16	18	20	22	24
3	3	6	9	12	15	18	21	24	27	30	33	36
4	4	8	12	16	20	24	28	32	36	40	44	48
5	5	10	15	20	25	30	35	40	45	50	55	60
6	6	12	18	24	30	36	42	48	54	60	66	72
7	7	14	21	28	35	42	49	56	63	70	77	84
8	8	16	24	32	40	48	56	64	72	80	88	96
9	9	18	27	36	45	54	63	72	81	90	99	108
10	10	20	30	40	50	60	70	80	90	100	110	120
11	11	22	33	44	55	66	77	88	99	110	121	132
12	12	24	36	48	60	72	84	96	108	120	132	144

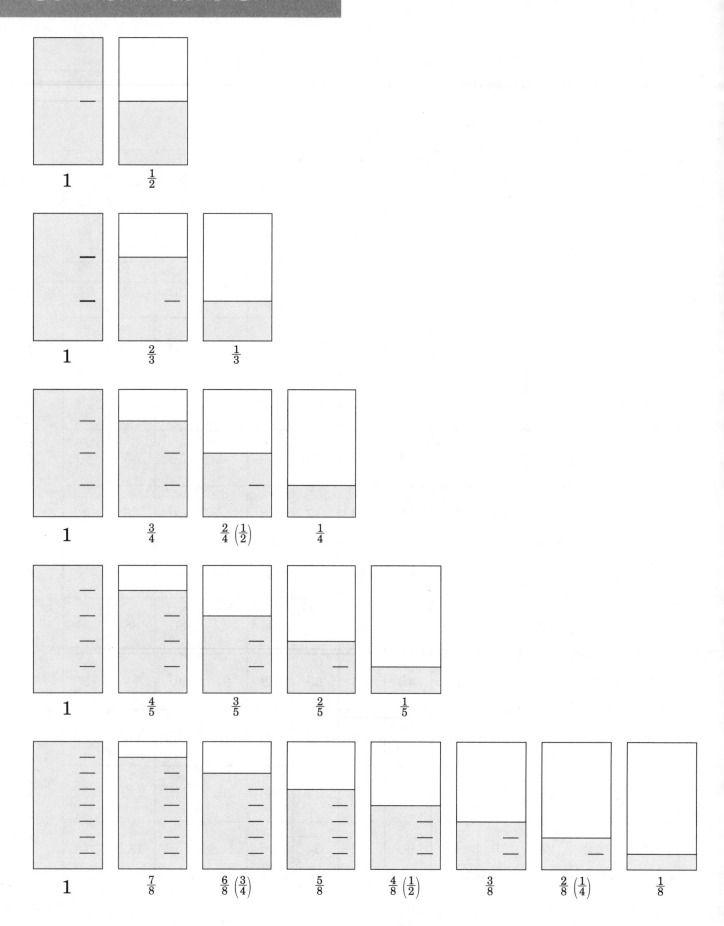